# MICROSOFT® VOICE AND
# UNIFIED COMMUNICATIONS

# MICROSOFT® VOICE AND UNIFIED COMMUNICATIONS

*Joe Schurman*

✦Addison-Wesley

Upper Saddle River, NJ • Boston • Indianapolis • San Francisco
New York • Toronto • Montreal • London • Munich • Paris • Madrid
Cape Town • Sydney • Tokyo • Singapore • Mexico City

Many of the designations used by manufacturers and sellers to distinguish their products are claimed as trademarks. Where those designations appear in this book, and the publisher was aware of a trademark claim, the designations have been printed with initial capital letters or in all capitals.

The author and publisher have taken care in the preparation of this book, but make no expressed or implied warranty of any kind and assume no responsibility for errors or omissions. No liability is assumed for incidental or consequential damages in connection with or arising out of the use of the information or programs contained herein.

The publisher offers excellent discounts on this book when ordered in quantity for bulk purchases or special sales, which may include electronic versions and/or custom covers and content particular to your business, training goals, marketing focus, and branding interests. For more information, please contact:

U.S. Corporate and Government Sales
(800) 382-3419
corpsales@pearsontechgroup.com

For sales outside the United States please contact:

International Sales
international@pearson.com

Visit us on the Web: informit.com/aw

*Library of Congress Cataloging-in-Publication Data:*

Schurman, Joe, 1977-
  Microsoft voice and unified communications / Joe Schurman.
    p. cm.
  ISBN 978-0-321-57995-9
  1. Internet telephony—Computer programs. 2. Multimedia communications—Computer programs. 3. Microsoft software. I. Title.

TK5105.8865.S368 2009
005.3—dc22

                                2008052525

Copyright © 2009 Pearson Education, Inc.

ISBN-13: 978-0-321-57995-9
ISBN-10: 0-321-57995-X

Text printed in the United States on recycled paper at R.R. Donnelley in Crawfordsville, Indiana.

First printing February 2009

Associate Publisher
Greg Wiegand

Acquisitions Editor
Loretta Yates

Development Editor
Kevin Howard

Managing Editor
Kristy Hart

Project Editor
Anne Goebel

Copy Editor
Geneil Breeze

Indexer
Erika Millen

Proofreader
Kathy Ruiz

Technical Reviewer
Tony Bradley

Publishing Coordinator
Cindy Teeters

Cover Designer
Gary Adair

Compositor
Gloria Schurick

*I dedicate this book to my wife, Christy, my three wonderful children, Paige, Bailey, and Davis, and to my friends and colleagues at Microsoft, as well as in the Microsoft partner community, who have challenged and helped me greatly throughout my career.*

# CONTENTS

# FOREWORD

The evolution of communications is a fascinating subject. From the primordial event where two people at the same place exchanged a single piece of semantically significant information to Gene Roddenberry's resplendent "Transporter" vision you have to wonder what were the incremental and disruptive steps—what endured and what did not. Like historians then, we use that thesis to predict what will work in the journey into the future of communications, and what will not.

In our lifetime the world has evolved from analog phone calls and telegraphs to PC-based communications. We have watched the PC and the Internet grow to reach more than a billion people in a span of 15 years or so. We have witnessed how the union of software and the Internet has become the jet fuel for the evolution of communications—creating an amalgamated medium for innovation and adoption unprecedented in the history of communications.

What we call **Unified Communications (UC)** is really the Renaissance of communications, in the same way the Renaissance period was for culture from the fourteenth century to the seventeenth century. UC is transforming the fundamentals—user experience, programmability, accessibility, reuse of components, and infrastructure. Everything is being and will continue to be challenged. The only thing sacred is the principle of empowering the end user with new capabilities offered within a cognitive model that is intuitive and practical.

Joe Schurman captures the essence of Microsoft's vision and implementation in the areas of voice and unified communications. This is an important book for those interested in connecting the dots between the present and the future in human communications and understanding why things are evolving in that way. Above all, this is a thorough and practical book, useful for those evaluating and planning the next step with Microsoft's Unified Communications offerings.

—Gurdeep Singh Pall,
Vice President, Microsoft Unified Communications Group

# PREFACE

The telecommunications industry is changing in ways not thought possible. We, as a human race, are seeing a complete transformation in how human communication can be used throughout applications and devices, truly connecting people and processes, regardless of geography, at a speed of innovation that is incomprehensible. The future of these successful innovations will lie within how human and machine-based communication will interact with tools that we use on a daily basis, liberating us from specific hardware and devices through the power of software. The purpose of this book is to introduce you to a company who is truly a leader in this strategy and vision and who is equipping the creative developers of tomorrow with the tools necessary to transform the world of voice and unified communications forever. This company is Microsoft Corporation, and the content within this book will help you understand what Microsoft is providing today and the vision for tomorrow throughout consumer, small business, and enterprise organizations on a global scale through the power of software.

# ACKNOWLEDGMENTS

I want to start by thanking my wife, Christy, and my children, Paige, Bailey, and Davis for their understanding of my time commitments to the research and writing of this book. I will definitely be catching up on many missed Xbox and PS3 games with Davis and spending time with the girls as well as a much needed series of nights out with the missus!

This book has most definitely been a fun and interesting project. Being the third book in my writing career, the process of writing was pretty easy. Loretta Yates, my editor at Pearson, was understanding of my demanding schedule, so I would like to thank Loretta and everyone at Pearson for their patience and assistance throughout this process. I also want to thank my assistant, Seth Neilson, who helped me in the imaging and graphic design process, and who is also the best graphic designer I know.

I also want to sincerely thank my mentors and career idols, Gurdeep Singh Pall and Xuedong (XD) Huang. I met Gurdeep years ago when working with the then RTC team when the only innovative feature we had was secure Instant Messaging. Gurdeep and his now vast team of engineers have really created an innovative platform as explained throughout this book in detail, and I am happy to have been involved in this program since the beginning deploying a market changing product with Live Communications Server 2003. In regards to XD, he is one of the most interesting and intelligent people I have ever met. Even though communication and conversation can be a bit scarce and difficult, XD has taught me a lot, and his team, including Rex Backman, Richard Sprague, John Wang, Ben Brauer, Robert Brown, Li Jiang, Regi John, Doug King, Chad Oftedal, Jay Waltmunson, Rita Zabolotskaya, and Marta Barillas have been incredible colleagues to work with. I also must not forget my initial buddies in the Microsoft Research Communications Innovation Center including JJ Cadiz, Veronica Buckley, Bob Taniguchi, and Jeff Smith plus many others. When I first walked into the Microsoft Research building in Redmond, Washington, I was definitely nervous in meeting some of the top IT minds on the planet, but everyone involved made me feel immediately welcome, and I have had a blast launching Response Point to the masses since the very beginning.

Many, many thanks to the partners who I work with in the UC and Response Point arena, including the Microsoft Response Point OEMs, including Yves LaLiberte, Francisco Palacios, Simon Beebe, and John Drolet at Aastra; Sam Liu at Quanta/Syspine; and Brian Nickell and Hendrik Hulleman at D-Link. Thanks also to the Microsoft UC partners I have worked with, including Baiju Jacob at Unisys; Randy Schrock via British Telecom; Chuck Rutledge, Pete Nelson, and Joanne Lowy at NET Quintum; Lior Moyal, Rose Chambers, Udi Cohen, and Rex Harris at AudioCodes; Sonu Aggarwal at Unify; Marcus Matthias, Allan MacGowan, and Ingrid Tremblay at Nortel; but especially, Eyal Inbar at NEC and Steve Given at Nortel.

I also want to thank my team at Evangelyze Communications who were extremely patient with me during this entire process. Creating a start-up enterprise services and development firm is not easy, and with the CEO writing a book at the same time, things can get a bit difficult and demanding, but my directors including Mike Stacy, Simon Booth, Tony Bradley, Ted Green, Rob Herman, and Satish Shah helped me out tremendously by virtually running the company when I had specific deadlines to meet for the book. Many thanks to such an innovative team, whose solutions are highlighted throughout the book as examples of voice and unified communications applications.

I thank my friends and colleagues, including my fellow Microsoft MVPs, including the original UC MVP duo with Thomas Wenzl and I, and the newer UC MVPs such as Lee, Thomas, Russell, John, Marshall, Bryan, Dennis, Arthur, and all the newcomers in the UC and Exchange MVP groups. I also thank my MVP lead, Melissa Travers, for her support and marketing of my contributions to the industry to Microsoft as well as Robin Martin-Emerson, my MVP liaison for the Unified Communications Group, who has included me in many behind-the-scenes meetings at Microsoft. Thanks also to my friends and colleagues at Microsoft, including Steve Erickson, Tim Stumbles, Cathy Sidwell, Matt Malloney, Roger Wilding, Bhushan Taravade, Darren Pryke, Maurice Milton, Ramin Vosough, Bill Baca, Dag Cummings, Ian Andrews, Neal Fiske, Tina Shepherd, Linda Roude, Oscar Newkirk, Anita Penders, Darcy Luer, Murari Narayan, Derek Whittle, Burke Fewel, Curtis Lee, Alisa Lahti, SV Purushothaman, Chris Wolff, Tom Moretti, Sanjay Patel, Barry Tannenbaum, Kevin Engman, Mark Nickerson, Greg Kastl, Sam Chon, Leigh Rubino, Chandler Bootchk, Jeremy Buch, Rui Maximo, Jerry Smith, Bob Maher, Rudy Campos, Meg Slesinger, Steve Chirico, Alex Wong,

Chris Chalmers, Chris Kunze, Rick Pinamonti, Paul Kiley, Grant Goodyear, Erin Simmons, Greg Smiley, Suhkvinder Singh Gulati, Shawn Pierce, Dennis Karlinski, Mu Hian, Mahendra Sekaran, Amey Parandekar, Ken Ewert, Kyle Marsh, Francois Doremieux, Albert Kooiman, Rui Maximo, Marc Sanders, Sean Olson, Jane Rasmussen, Sanjay Patel, and especially David Alexander, my brother from another mother, and Jack Lyons for those many sushi lunches. Apologies to those I have forgotten!

I also would like to thank JD Holzgrefe, Matt Morollo, Pat Davis, and Doug Barney at Redmond Media Group and am looking forward to exposing more Microsoft Voice and Unified Communications content through this venue.

Finally, I want to thank my extended family including my grandfather, George Schurman, for all of his support personally and his investments in my company, Evangelyze Communications; my father, Rankin Schurman, and brother, Brenton Schurman, who assisted me greatly during this process by dealing with company investments in my firm as they were the only people I could trust to do this while my time was spent writing this book. I also want to thank my mother, Larin, who, along with my father, gave me the gifted gene of loving to write. Thanks also to my mother-in-law, Debbie Davis, who gave me my first start in the IT industry those many years ago at Compaq Computer Corporation, and my father-in-law, Johnny Davis, for all of his assistance, guidance, and love.

# ABOUT THE AUTHOR

**Joe Schurman**, the founder of Evangelyze Communications, is an internationally renowned expert and speaker for voice and unified communications technologies. Joe has provided speaking engagements to audiences on every continent, and his research, development, and publications have been highly regarded. Mr. Schurman's articles and speeches have been published in online, print, and media syndications globally, and he is also a published author as well as a regular columnist for Redmond Media Group. Mr. Schurman provides private consulting to Microsoft and Nortel executives with strategic and innovative marketing and technical research. Mr. Schurman also provides one-on-one presentations and briefings to CxO-level executives of Fortune 500 and Global 500 organizations to present and introduce new innovations in voice and unified communications technologies. Mr. Schurman holds several awards including the Microsoft Gold Presenter Award and is a five-time Microsoft Most Valuable Professional (MVP) Award winner. Prior to founding Evangelyze Communications, Mr. Schurman, who began his career with Hewlett-Packard, founded and sold other organizations, was a managing consultant of the Microsoft Solutions Organization of Accenture, a senior technology architect for IBM, and a senior technology officer of Chase Manhattan Bank.

# CHAPTER 1

# THE COMMUNICATIONS RENAISSANCE

## Telephony Revolution

Fast forward to the near future—to the year 2010. I just finished yet another training seminar. Sweating a bit from all the excitement and talking, tired from standing all day, and a bit hoarse, I walk back to my hotel and at the same time, join a late afternoon conference call with one of my colleagues, Seth. Instead of just holding the phone up to my face generating even more heat, I am having a live video and voice conversation with him on my new mobile phone (see Figure 1.1).

**FIGURE 1.1** Mobile video call

We wrap up the conference call and then I head up to the hotel to finish out the day with a cold one overlooking the European-esque architecture of beautiful Buenos Aires, Argentina, where I had been before.

Now, rewind to the last time I gave a speech in Argentina in the days before VoIP became prominently available. That is a much different story. After my speech, I wanted to call my wife, but I realized I did not have a phone connection—not even a roaming connection! There I was on my US, unstandardized CDMA phone in a GSM-supported location of Argentina with no phone access—none! I ended up walking through the pouring rain to the nearest mobile phone store to purchase a pay-as-you-go phone with a new SIM card running on the Personal network there in Buenos Aires. After slogging through water up to my ankles back to my hotel, I tried to make the call. After several failed dialing attempts and several calls to a Spanish-speaking only network service line, I learned that that the pay-as-you-go phone did not have the ability to make international calls, so the entire adventure was all for naught. In the end, I used the hotel phone to make the hundred-dollar call to my wife (see Figure 1.2).

**FIGURE 1.2** Perfect depiction of how I felt

Now, back to the near future in my mobile video conference with Seth! I'm not sweating at all thinking about the past situation because now, the video and voice call I just made, unlike before, was covered in my $29 USD per month plan. No wireless PSTN surcharge, no $100 USD per month wireless plan, no international roaming, no GSM, CDMA, 3G, and so on. My new wireless broadband phone that has HD-video and crystal clear HD-audio with no interruption is leveraging a technology made available for consumer use in the 1990s called **Voice over Internet Protocol (VoIP)**.

That's right! VoIP has been around for more than a decade! What's most important to note is that somewhere, some business executive who works for a wireless provider or telecommunications (Telco) provider is starting to sweat. Why? Because this executive is beginning to realize what is happening—the end of wireless and wireline communications services as they exist today. No more SIM cards, no more international roaming, no more dictatorship! For more than three decades telecommunications providers have, similarly to how energy companies have, controlled the cost and service to their consumer and commercial customers by charging whatever rates and fees they want at will.

No more!

This time marks the beginning of the end of traditional telecommunication services and the provider's ability to enforce unjust fees and limitations to its customers. This is the birth of a new world of telecommunications leveraging the power of voice and unified communications software! Your charter is to understand what this change means and prepare for what is to come.

For the past two decades many organizations have designed and developed technologies that leverage voice and unified communications, but have failed miserably, or they have introduced these services before thoroughly testing them for mass use. This has in some cases given VoIP a bad name, which is why my book is not entitled, Microsoft VoIP, but Microsoft Voice and Unified Communications. The purpose of this book is to identify the most innovative voice and unified communications provider on a global basis and its products and services for consumers, small businesses, and enterprise organizations.

You may know already that providers are developing new voice and unified communications technology to change the way we communicate forever, and for the better. Some typical names are Nortel, Cisco, Avaya, and other leading providers in the telecommunications industry. What you may not realize is that a company based out of Redmond, Washington that is popular in the area of software development and manufacturing will forever shape the future of voice-based communication and collaboration technology. This company's name is Microsoft, and the purpose of this book is to provide insight into what these technologies are and to prepare you for the next wave of communications innovation.

## Telephony Evolution

To understand how Microsoft's Voice and Unified Communications vision will change the telecommunications industry, it's first important to understand how the telecommunications industry has evolved. I love how some movies or books start with a "In the beginning...." In keeping with tradition, I will also say, "In the beginning, there was **Plain Old Telephone Service (POTS)**." POTS was the first communications layer to enable one person to talk to another without having to ride a horse, fly a plane, or drive a car to see someone in person. Some say that this was the beginning of the end in human communication in that we are now seeing more and more individuals hiding behind the phone and spending less time in person, which I completely agree with, but hope to live in a time where we can evolve communications to enforce visual presence. However, POTS enabled the first wave of communications. End users of a POTS line would use a first edition phone device, designed and manufactured by Alexander Graham Bell himself, to communicate to the same type of device held by another end user with a POTS phone (see Figure 1.3).

**FIGURE 1.3** POTS (analog) line

Lines were terminated by switches, which soon led to a release of a new technology launched in the vibrant 1970s, the **Public Switch Telephone Network (PSTN)**, which enabled a company, remember Ma Bell, to terminate calls to enable long-distance calling internationally. Back then, we all paid, well, you paid, because I was too young to have a phone in my own name, exorbitant fees at each termination resulting in an expensive phone bill if long distance was used. Basically the PSTN connected POTS phones across cities, states, countries, and ultimately oceans to enable voice packets to be sent and received across PSTN networks in each region of the world (see Figure 1.4).

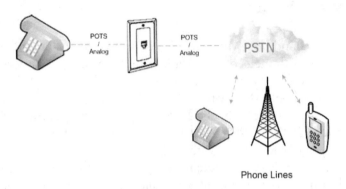

**FIGURE 1.4** POTS/PSTN integration

Within the same decade, **Private Branch eXchange (PBX)** systems, illustrated in Figure 1.5, were released to enable corporations to host their own telephone network without having to pay for individual POTS lines for each office worker. PBX telephone users would call each other using a four- or seven- digit extension, and if they had to dial one of the enabled outside POTS lines, they would normally dial a 9 and then the number. Remember dialing 9 at school to call home? Yep, that's where this comes from. Anyway, POTS lines are shared within the PBX network so that 16 to 20 employees may use eight POTS lines in a given company, and that's how most PBX systems are still sold today in an 8x16 model. PBX systems connect to PSTN systems as well as connect PBX phones to long-distance callers.

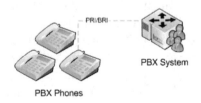

**FIGURE 1.5** Private Branch eXchange

1. THE COMMUNICATIONS RENAISSANCE

Around the 1990s, PBX and PSTN systems and networks started to accept digital voice packets. By accepting digital packets, PBX systems were able to advance using **Internet Protocol (IP)** communications connecting voice over the Internet and creating a new way to communicate using what we now know as VoIP. VoIP is a protocol or a vessel by which communications including voice, video, and data pass over an IP line. VoIP uses another protocol called **Session Initiation Protocol (SIP**; see Figure 1.6) to pass this data. (This will be important for you to remember later.)

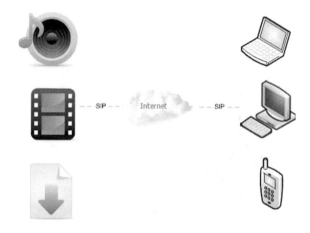

**FIGURE 1.6** Session Initiation Protocol

What is needed for this to work? Simple, an Internet connection. With new Wi-Fi and WiMax technology, obtaining an Internet connection is easier and more broad reaching than ever before, and in the future, Internet connections will blanket the earth. PSTN networks are also crucial in this development as voice calls are carried from a VoIP service provider, known as an **Internet Telephony Service Provider (ITSP)** to the PSTN using digital packets to terminate a connection to a POTS line as well as cellular/mobile lines.

As depicted in Figure 1.7, PBX systems can take advantage of this because they can now utilize SIP as the primary communications layer for external communication instead of having to rely on POTS or analog lines. Internally, PBX systems also upgraded their service protocols by moving away from **Primary Rate Interface (PRI)** and **Binary Rate Interface (BRI)** lines to IP-based Ethernet-enabled cabling, creating the IP-PBX as we know today.

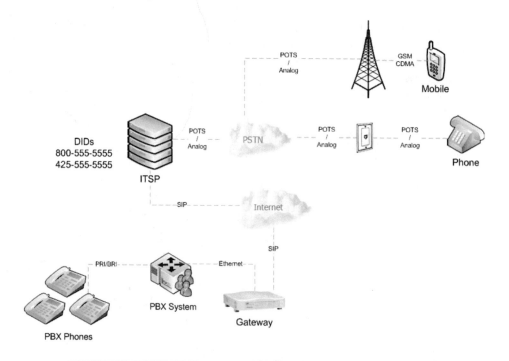

**FIGURE 1.7** PBX/SIP integrated architecture

## SIP'ing VoIP

VoIP services and IP-based communications services, such as the IP-PBX, leverage protocols to carry audio, video, and data. The two most popular VoIP protocols are H.323 and SIP. For detail on these protocols, visit the **Internet Engineering Task Force (IETF)** via its Web site at http://www.ietf.org searching for RFC 2543 for SIP, and the **International Telecommunications Union (ITU-T)** Web site via http://www.itu.int for details on H.323. As depicted in the figures earlier in this chapter, SIP is the standard VoIP protocol used to carry audio, video, and data communications and is the protocol that Microsoft chose to build its communication platform of products on due to the ability to provide more flexibility and customization in how audio, video, and data are handled between applications (see Figure 1.8). H.323 was the previous industry standard, but based on its rigidness and lack of flexibility, was not the protocol of choice. Another major reason why H.323 was not chosen has to do with bandwidth. The goal of VoIP is to work within ubiquitous networks and lower the overall threshold of the communication pipe to lower bandwidth requirements enabling lightweight applications and devices that leverage VoIP.

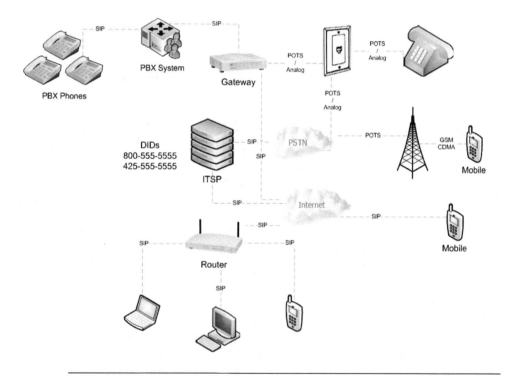

**FIGURE 1.8** SIP architecture

Leveraging SIP as the foundation protocol for VoIP enables Microsoft to build communications products that carry the richness of audio, video, and data as well as provide the capability of custom application development to enhance these SIP-based products using third-party integrated solutions from Microsoft's worldwide partner community. In the future, as expressed in my hypothetical 2010 scenario described earlier in this chapter, these flexible and feature-rich solutions will be extended to mobile users leveraging SIP over wireless broadband networks such as WiMax towers that spread a broadband Internet connection across entire regions. Like you see in Japan and in spy movies, you will be able to communicate, via mobile, audio, video, and data without using your mobile wireless carrier network, saving you time and at a fraction of the cost.

## The Presence of SIP

Leveraging SIP further, Microsoft, unlike its competitors including Cisco and IBM, has taken a different approach in respect to providing voice communications services to its customers. Microsoft has built its services around the core human element, presence (see Figure 1.9). Understanding Microsoft's focus on presence, its vision of human-based presence services, will unlock the understanding of Microsoft's vision of future communications and collaboration services. Think about this for a minute. Telco and networking providers have built communications technologies based on the technology itself, not considering the human element. They have confined you as an individual and companies to the actual service itself and then have built enhancements on top of this service. Microsoft took another approach. Microsoft thought about you, the individual. What good is the technology if you are not there to use it? What good is the technology if it cannot adapt to you as a person? The Discovery channel has a series called *How It's Made*, which focuses on the manufacturing of consumer goods from crayons to baseball bats to even popsicles. These machines have advanced cameras that can sort items based on color and size. These cameras identify motion and color, and are sensitive to the touch of the item as well. Why can't technology like this be applied to the way we communicate? When I wake up in the morning and rise out of bed, why can't a camera or sensor be educated/programmed enough to sense my presence, my schedule, or even my health and determine what services I need in respect to contacts I can communicate with or meet with, or even to see whether I'm feeling blue? No other manufacturer of communications-based technologies is focusing on the human element. One company in particular is advertising this focus, but it is simply advertising. Microsoft is actually walking the walk without the hype and advertisement.

**FIGURE 1.9** SIP/Presence

They have focused their communications and collaboration products based on the human element, based on human presence; and out of this foundation, they have built additional services on top. The focus on this core, critical human element, will far surpass any of its competitors as technology changes in that the core will remain the same, providing the ability to add better performing and functioning applications and hardware surrounding presence. By focusing the development of these products on the foundation of presence-based communications, Microsoft will outwit its competitors "hand over fist."

Leveraging this presence-based model as identified in the RFC 3856 documentation, which can be found via http://www.ietf.org/, enables Microsoft applications to integrate with telephony equipment such as phone devices and PBX systems. The presence-based model also works with applications to provide better insight to users on a contacts list to identify each other's true availability as mentioned earlier in the form of presence status indicators such as Away, Busy, Online, or Offline, which are the standard, but also extend to On the Phone, In a Conference, and In a Meeting as well as customized presence functionality so you can configure your own, such as "Gone Fishing." Regardless, this focus on presence is the central core of Microsoft's portfolio of voice and unified communications products and services for the future, benefiting the actual user of the technology to increase productivity and enhance collaboration capabilities.

## The Battle for Voice Quality

Even though IP-based communications have matured since the 1990s, many organizations and individuals are still skeptical in relying on VoIP for reasons such as dependence on power and the quality of the service compared to traditional telephony services, put simply, the analog dial tone. Since Microsoft's entry into the Unified Communications marketplace, the question of voice quality was the primary target of Microsoft's competitors, specifically Cisco. Telecommunication providers such as Cisco, Avaya, Nortel, and others sell **Quality of Service (QoS)** along with their devices and application platforms. QoS networking routers and switches provide compression on the codecs that are used to transmit the audio that initiates from one phone to the other or one PBX to the other. These existing telephony players use legacy codecs as well, which force them to use QoS devices and services to ensure that the quality of the call is clear. For example, the audio codec used for SIP calling is G.711. For more detailed information about this codec, visit the ITU Web site via http://itu.int. The PBX uses this codec at a rate of 64KB per second to transmit the audio. The telephony provider will usually provide a QoS router that keeps this compression low to make sure that disturbances such as jitter, lossless audio, and echoing do not occur during the transmission. Bottom line, telephony providers are obsessed with this feature, and for good reason, but it seems to be the only thing they are obsessed with outside of raping the customer with overpriced, unnecessary hardware.

Microsoft took a different approach to QoS by adding **Quality of Experience (QoE)** to the equation. To explain QoE, you need to know that all Unified Communications providers, including Microsoft, use **Mean of Opinion (MOS)** scores to determine the measurement of quality of the communications infrastructure. MOS can be used for video and voice as well. Table 1.1 outlines an example of a MOS score report covering many different codecs within a company's telephony environment.

**Table 1.1** MOS Scores

| Codec | Kilobytes/Second | MOS Score |
|---|---|---|
| G.711 (ISDN) | 64 | 4.3 |
| iLBC | 15.2 | 4.14 |
| AMR | 12.2 | 4.14 |
| G.729 | 8 | 3.92 |
| G.723.1r63 | 6.3 | 3.9 |
| GSM EFR | 12.2 | 3.8 |
| G.726 ADPCM | 32 | 3.8 |
| G.729a | 8 | 3.7 |
| G.723.1r53 | 5.3 | 3.65 |
| GSM FR | 12.2 | 3.5 |

Source: http://en.wikipedia.org/wiki/Mean_opinion_score

MOS scores are rated between a range of 1 and 5 based on categories of rating in Table 1.2.

**Table 1.2** MOS Score Ratings

| MOS | Quality | Impairment |
|---|---|---|
| 5 | Excellent | Imperceptible |
| 4 | Good | Perceptible but not annoying |
| 3 | Fair | Slightly annoying |
| 2 | Poor | Annoying |
| 1 | Bad | Very annoying |

Source: http://en.wikipedia.org/wiki/Mean_opinion_score

Microsoft took this a step further by adding QoE to not only provide quality of the communications service from a networking perspective, but also from a user experience perspective. While QoS looks only at the hard evidence of the system, QoE factors in the actual user experience. This means that even though the QoS reports may be perfect, some of the users within the same reported environment may still experience static or some other kind of line trouble, so the QoS may result overall in a good score, but bottom line the service is still not operational, especially if the CEO is the user experiencing the line interference. Microsoft created its own QoE Monitoring Server that diagnoses and collects reports on the experience of each communication endpoint (see Figure 1.10). As soon as a call or session is completed, reports and statistics are sent to the server and are available for review. Metrics are taken in real time during each user session so that the true user experience is captured to ensure the quality of the overall service.

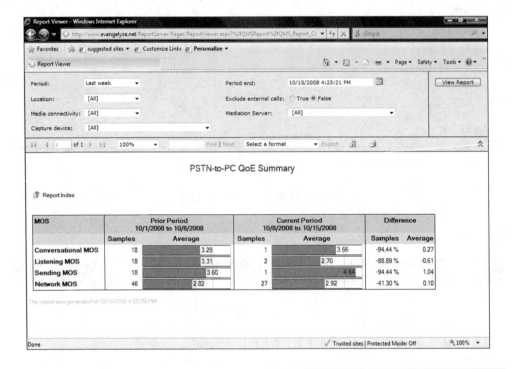

FIGURE 1.10 An example of a QoE report generated from the Microsoft QoE Monitoring Server

## Voice Protocols and Codecs

Rounding out this introduction of voice and unified communications concepts, we now take a look at which protocols are used that provide the audio, video, and data experience. So far, I have mentioned SIP, which is used as the protocol for audio, video, and data. Another key protocol used by VoIP that is important to understand is **Real-time Transport Protocol (RTP)**. RTP works with both H.323 and SIP, explained earlier in this chapter, and was originally created as the standard protocol used for VoIP. RTP is the delivery mechanism that carries audio and video over an IP network as well as the Internet.

In addition to VoIP protocols, as mentioned earlier in the QoS/QoE discussion, codecs are used to provide the actual band of voice communication. The most popular of which, and Microsoft designed, **Real-time Audio (RTAudio)** is a wide-band speech codec used by Microsoft's voice communications products to compress the speech/audio used in a multi-person or two-way conversation (see Figure 1.11).

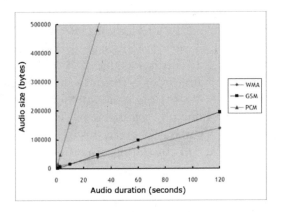

**FIGURE 1.11** An example of RTAudio sample rates

This level of audio compression gives Microsoft the competitive advantage over traditional Telco providers in that the audio compression provided by the RTAudio codec ensures nonpacket loss, which ultimately means less or no jitter on the line. RTAudio is susceptible to delays, though, which is why QoS and QoE are used to overcompensate for any flaws that may be present within this voice communication infrastructure.

## Securing Voice Communications

There are many areas where voice and unified communications can be secured, depending on the level of security needed by specific organizations. Chapter 8, "Securing Voice," explains this security information in more detail. There is the filtering of bad traffic in the form of viruses and buffer overflows as well as the identification and encryption of SIP communication between servers and clients. Microsoft offers security for both models, using its Microsoft Forefront security product line for filtering attacks, viruses, and SPIM, which is SPAM for Instant Messaging and if it finds its way into your network, say hello to the most annoying experience of your IT administrative life. To encrypt the communications, SIP uses **Transport Layer Security (TLS)**. More detailed information on TLS can be found via the IETF Web site at http://www.ietf.org under the RFC 2246. TLS is an evolution of **Secured Sockets Layer (SSL)**, which is heavily used in the configuration of Web site and e-commerce applications online. Both require certificates that are generated from a **Certificate Authority (CA)**. A CA can be private or public, meaning you can use the CA service provided within an internal Microsoft Windows Server environment to generate certificates for your internal SIP servers. An example of a public CA would be providers such as VeriSign, Entrust, and even GoDaddy that generate certificates that are widely trusted and are already installed as preconfigured root certificates on every new PC and Mac as well as on mobile devices such as Windows Mobile and Blackberry devices.

TLS uses an architecture that includes a CA that generates a root certificate trust and also generates certificates for servers and clients that trust against the root CA. This brokering of certificates as depicted in Figure 1.12 enables a VoIP/SIP environment to establish secure sessions between servers and between clients.

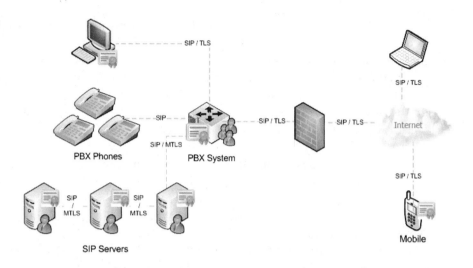

**FIGURE 1.12** TLS/MTLS architecture

To provide security between servers exclusively, the use of **Mutual Transport Layer Security (MTLS)** certificates configure a trust between VoIP/SIP servers. Within the Microsoft Unified Communications infrastructure itself, Microsoft enforces the use of TLS and MTLS to ensure that the UC servers that communicate with one another and clients that communicate with these servers, between each other, and between federated partners or public ITSP networks, are trusted and secure.

## The Microsoft Vision of Software-Powered Voice

As mentioned earlier, Microsoft has taken the software approach to providing voice and unified communications products instead of relying on hardware devices such as PBX systems and phone devices to make these innovative end-user communication features usable.

Building off Microsoft-designed and industry standards-based protocols and codecs, combined with learning from the mistakes of traditional Telco manufacturers and injecting some of the industry's top voice and unified communications product specialists, Microsoft has the opportunity to take voice services, applications, and devices to an entirely new level.

What inspires me the most about Microsoft's vision for voice and unified communications solutions has to do with the determination to build an open platform, but also to design and develop new technologies, including applications and devices. But most inspiring are the underlying voice protocols, codecs, and the obsessiveness to ensure the quality of these services to provide customers a high-fidelity, price conscious, and adaptable voice solution despite the size of the customer. My vision of where Microsoft will clearly succeed in the areas of voice and unified communications technologies is within the focus of software plus services. Many of Microsoft's competitors are busy designing the latest and greatest switches, conferencing devices, phones, and headsets. To be completely honest, this technology is archaic and rudimentary. What will change the way people truly communicate over the next 5 to 10 years lies within the ability to transform voice through applications. My vision is that we will be able to develop line-of-business and vertical industry applications that will completely change the way business processes are executed and will provide organizations with the ability to provide services that make a difference in the way humans communicate and collaborate in a way that is not yet understandable. The only true leader in this space, the only company focused on providing visionary developers and strategic organizations with the tools to build these innovative voice solutions, is clearly and always has been Microsoft Corporation. The focus on software, the ability to integrate voice and unified communications into applications, and the future of these technologies will enable an experience that crosses devices, applications, Web sites, mobility, and virtualization like we have never seen before, and this all comes down to one fundamental aspect, human presence. We will now explore these technological breakthroughs in more detail to give you a better understanding of what is ahead and how to prepare for the coming Communications Renaissance!

# CHAPTER 2

# CONSUMER VOICE COMMUNICATIONS WITH WINDOWS LIVE

There is a common myth that Microsoft does not care about the consumer and only focuses on its commercial customers. In reality, the converse is true. Television commercials such as Apple Computer's Mac Guy versus PC Guy, which I do think are hilarious, further position Microsoft as a lame, non-hip entity. To be honest, Microsoft is the most consumer-focused software company in the industry and has been for decades. Apple comes in a close third behind Google. And I'm not biased as I am using Microsoft Office 2008 to write this book on my Mac Book Air, so shush! The reason Microsoft is sometimes viewed as a dud is because their consumer marketing division is flat-out inexperienced and disconnected from the world, as proven with the confusing Vista and Zune advertisements. Unfortunately, Microsoft's cool marketing is portrayed only online so consumers have no idea about the applications that Microsoft provides at no cost to consumers. Such is the case with a free, consumer-focused, state-of-the-art presence-based voice communication software product called Windows Live Messenger, formerly known as MSN Messenger.

Since the release of MSN Messenger in the late 1990s, Microsoft has made significant advances to this product which, as of this writing, is in version 8 of its Windows Live Messenger client. Through the addition of part-nered voice services by companies such as Telefonica and soon Intercall, Microsoft provides consumers with a beautiful voice-enabled application through Windows Live Messenger that provides features such as Instant Messaging (IM), video, audio, file sharing, desktop sharing, remote computer/desktop support, and VoIP services such as the ability to call to a wireline phone service such as a home or business analog line, connection to a wireless provider, or direct connection to another Windows Live Messenger or non-Microsoft products such as the Yahoo! Messenger client.

**FIGURE 2.1** Microsoft Windows Live Messenger

Through this aesthetically pleasing application, Windows Live Messenger provides an intuitive approach, based on presence, to enable quick access to instantly message or provide a video and/or voice call to another contact. With one click, you can share thoughts, files, and contacts. Personally, I travel quite often on behalf of Microsoft or for my own business. When I am sent to provide speeches on tour, I can be gone for weeks on end, ranging from Seattle to Singapore. On my second global speaking tour for Microsoft, my wife and children were not taking the travel well and I had to do something to establish contact. I was only able to do this successfully through Windows Live Messenger. Through a 2–3 second operation, we were able to see and hear each other, which aided us greatly in those depressing moments. There is a marketing slogan for you: "Windows Live Messenger saved my family"!

**FIGURE 2.2** My family via Microsoft Windows Live Messenger

Let's take a test drive of Windows Live Messenger so that you can see for yourself how cool this application is. Through this process, I will help you set up your Windows Live Messenger Account, we'll play with some of the features, test out the voice calling service, and you will soon agree how consumer-focused Microsoft can be.

## Setting Up a Windows Live Messenger Account

Installing and setting up a Windows Live Messenger account is simple. To start, follow these steps.

For PC users:

1. Go to http://get.live.com.
2. Follow the instructions to download the Windows Live Messenger application.
3. Browse to the directory on your computer where you downloaded the setup file.

4. Double-click the setup file to install and follow the prompts to finalize the installation.

5. After the installation process is complete, you are asked to sign in to the application using a Windows Live ID (see Figure 2.3). If you are new to Windows Live, follow the link that asks you to register; it's free!

6. After you successfully sign in to the service, you then have access to all the features within Windows Live Messenger.

**FIGURE 2.3** Microsoft Windows Live Messenger login

For Mac users:

1. To access Windows Live contacts and services on a Mac, you need to download and install Mac Messenger (see Figure 2.4). To do so, visit http://www.microsoft.com/download.

2. In the search bar, type in **Mac Messenger**.
3. Select the latest version of Mac Messenger, which at the time of this writing is 7.1.
4. After downloading, run the installation file image on your Mac and then sign in using your Windows Live ID. As stated previously, if you do not have a Windows Live ID, either register using the Mac Messenger client or go to http://get.live.com to register for an account.

**FIGURE 2.4** Microsoft Messenger for Mac login

## Signing Up for VoIP Service

All the peer-to-peer communication features within Windows Live Messenger and Mac Messenger are free. To enable VoIP service, you must sign up for a voice provider through the client service. Today, Microsoft uses Telefonica to provide VoIP service for Windows Live Messenger only. Mac Messenger for Personal Contacts currently does not support video or voice communications.

To sign up for VoIP service within Windows Live Messenger, follow these steps:

1. Within Windows Live Messenger, choose the menu from the drop-down arrow on the top right-hand corner of the application.
2. From the menu select Tools, Billing Information, Phone Calls, as shown in Figure 2.5.

**FIGURE 2.5** Microsoft Windows Live Messenger tools menu

3. You are then taken to a Web site where you have the option of signing up for new voice service through Telefonica. Decide on a plan that makes sense for you (see Figure 2.6).

**FIGURE 2.6** Microsoft Windows Live Call VoIP account setup

4. Once completed you can now use Windows Live Messenger for voice calls.

## Adding Contacts

Adding your messaging contacts using Windows Live Messenger is a breeze. Once your contacts are added, you can view their presence; communicate with them via voice, video, and Instant Messaging; share emotions using emoticons or purchased winks; and more. You can also manage your contacts within groups to easily see who's available and who isn't with a blink of an eye.

To add contacts using Windows Live Messenger, follow these steps:

1. From the main window, you can either use the Find a Contact search bar or choose the green-colored buddy icon adjacent to the contact search bar or even use the menu as described in the previous section by choosing Contacts, Add a Contact.
2. In the Add a Contact menu, type in the IM address of the contact you are trying to add; for example:
   **joe.schurman@messengeruser.com** (see Figure 2.7).

**FIGURE 2.7** Contact information

3. You can choose to fill out the additional contact details within this window or just click on the Add Contact button located in the bottom right-hand corner of the window.

To add a contact group, follow these steps:

1. Using the Windows Live Messenger menu as described previously, select Contacts, Create a Group.

2. In the Enter a Group Name field shown in Figure 2.8, enter the name of the group that you want to create.

**FIGURE 2.8** Group contacts selection

3. Select the contacts in the provided list of contacts on the screen to add these contacts to the group and then click the Save button.

## Communicating with a Contact

Now that you are registered, signed in, and hopefully have a few contacts, let's collaborate. Use the following steps to invoke communications with a Windows Live Messenger contact:

1. Start by using Instant Messaging. Check to see whether your contact is online by viewing his Presence icon. If the icon is green, that means that the person is available (see Figure 2.9).

**FIGURE 2.9** Contact presence (availability)

2. Now, send an Instant Message to the contact by double-clicking on the contact's name in the contact list.

3. After the messaging window is up, you can begin typing text into it. Type in the words, **Do you want to start a video call?** as shown in Figure 2.10 and then press the Return or Enter button on your keyboard.

4. If your contact responds with an acceptance, using your mouse, click on the Video Call icon within the messaging window as shown in Figure 2.11.

5. Your contact now receives an invitation for this video call. After your contact accepts, Windows Live Messenger automatically uses your webcam to show your video and your speakers and microphone to transmit and receive your audio/voice. Play around with this call and test the video and audio capabilities, noticing that you can still send instant messages back and forth during the call.

**FIGURE 2.10** Instant messaging session

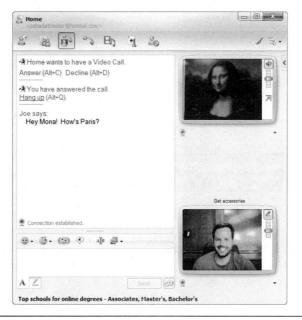

**FIGURE 2.11** Video conversation

6. You can now end the session by closing the messaging window using the X button on the top right-hand corner of the window.

This was a good example of how easy it is to use peer-to-peer communications using Windows Live Messenger. Now, let's use the built-in VoIP services to place an actual voice call over the Internet to a phone. For testing purposes, you can use your wireline or wireless phone as the external caller. Follow these steps to complete this scenario:

1. In the Windows Live Messenger main menu, choose Actions, Call, Call a Phone, as shown in Figure 2.12.

FIGURE 2.12 Placing a voice call

2.  The Windows Live Call window now appears. From within this window you can sign up for VoIP service in the lower right-hand corner of the Window, view tips on how to use the calling features, and review your call history, but we focus on placing an actual call. In the Call section of the window, just above the digital phone keypad that you would normally see on an actual phone, there is a blank box. In this box, type the phone number of your mobile or landline. Make sure to include the country code. For the United States, it's 1.

3.  After you enter the number, choose the Call button on the bottom right-hand corner of the Call section

4.  Windows Live Call now attempts a call to the number you provided, and your phone should ring (see Figure 2.13).

**FIGURE 2.13** Windows Live Call

5.  You will now use the computer's speakers and microphone to speak and hear yourself from your phone. It's as simple as that.

## Collaborating Using Microsoft Messenger for Mac

Using Windows Live through the Microsoft Messenger client for the Mac is just as easy as on the PC. The only downfall to this solution currently is the lack of video and voice collaboration. What's cool about this package, if you downloaded it based on the instructions earlier in this chapter, is that the Microsoft Messenger for Mac comes with two clients as shown in Figure 2.14—one for Windows Live and the other for corporate access through Microsoft's enterprise Unified Communications platform, which I explain in Chapter 4, "Enterprise Voice with Microsoft Unified Communications."

**FIGURE 2.14** Microsoft Messenger for Mac (personal and corporate)

To collaborate via Instant Messaging through the Mac's version of this solution is simple. All you have to do after signing in to the client application is find a contact based on her availability or presence as shown in Figure 2.15.

Then simply contact that individual by clicking on the person's name as shown in the Figure 2.16.

**FIGURE 2.15** Microsoft Messenger for Mac (personal contacts)

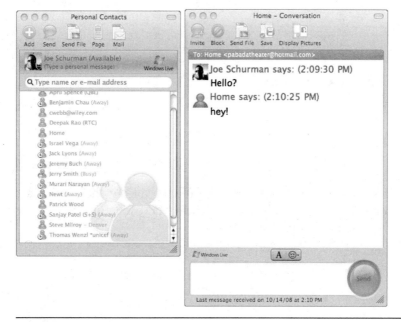

**FIGURE 2.16** Instant message conversation

Another cool feature enabled in the Mac Messenger client for Windows Live is paging. If a contact specifies a phone number in his contact information such as a mobile number that can accept pages, you can page a contact directly from the client and enter a phone number or test message to send as depicted in Figure 2.17.

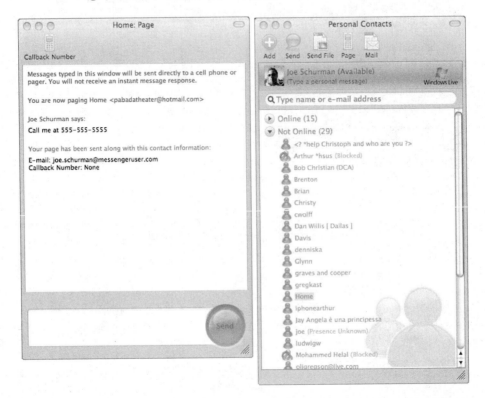

**FIGURE 2.17** Paging feature

Leveraging this innovative product via the slick and cool Mac OS X operating system only further proves Microsoft's interop story with even its biggest PC competitor.

# Windows Live Call Voice Architecture

You might ask how it was possible to place a voice call to your mobile or landline phone from Windows Live Messenger/Windows Live Call. Well, it's not as complex as you think. Remember when I introduced SIP? Just as a reminder, SIP is the protocol that carries voice, video, and data communications for VoIP applications and devices. With the power of VoIP, you can use an application such as Windows Live Call as a SIP client that connects to a SIP server. In this case you are using Windows Live Messenger's Windows Live Call application, which is the SIP client. You use this SIP client to communicate with the Windows Live Call service, which is the SIP server. This SIP server then connects through the VoIP or ITSP provider's service; in this case, we are using Telefonica. The ITSP then translates the call to the PSTN, which is the public phone network if you remember from earlier. The PSTN then sends your translated call to your phone device where you then pick up and speak back and forth through this SIP to PSTN connection (see Figure 2.18).

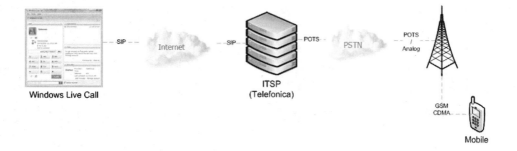

**FIGURE 2.18** Windows Live Call architecture

This is a prime example of the power of VoIP. Now why is Microsoft different from other software manufacturers in respect to VoIP application development? Integration is your answer. What's great about Microsoft's approach to VoIP is that outside of basing the foundation of these applications, such as Windows Live Messenger, on Presence, these features are integrated with the desktop, your day-to-day experience. Within the Microsoft Office suite or by browsing a Web site using Internet Explorer, you have the capability of seeing the presence or availability of other contacts as well as directly communicate from within these applications providing you with a connected environment. This was Bill Gates' vision when he first announced the release of .NET technology from Microsoft a decade ago. We now have the capability of connecting applications, services, and people better than ever before. And this is just a start.

To summarize, Microsoft has provided amazingly innovative products to consumers. Using Microsoft Windows Live Messenger as an example of this ability from a voice perspective only shows that Microsoft can provide an innovative voice client for little or no cost at all to connect people on a global basis without charging them a dime. Over the next few chapters, we will discuss how this same innovative approach is applied plus more for small- and medium-sized businesses, as well as enterprise organizations through Microsoft's market leading voice and unified communications products.

# CHAPTER 3

# SMALL BUSINESS VOICE COMMUNICATIONS WITH MICROSOFT RESPONSE POINT

Filling the gap between consumers and enterprise customers, a small business group inside Microsoft Research (MSR), now called the Communications Innovation Center (CIC), which is part of the Microsoft Startup Business Accelerator program, gave birth to a new, highly innovative, small business IP phone system in 2007. Using existing Microsoft voice technologies such as speech recognition through award-winning products such as Microsoft Speech Server and voice communication and collaboration solutions such as the Microsoft Unified Communications platform, the CIC built a best-of-breed IP phone system with Microsoft Response Point targeting a small business user base of 50 phones or less. Response Point packs an enormous punch at an affordable price to small businesses as well as Small office/Home office (SoHo) organizations, killing the existing competition.

For years, small business customers have turned to Cisco, Avaya, Nortel, and Panasonic, to name a few, for their small business phone system needs and have experienced the pain of spending tens of thousands of dollars in phone hardware plus additional funds for licensing fees to leverage the voice, voicemail, and integrated VoIP services.

Over the past several years, customers have also tried using hybrid IP phone systems also known as virtual Private Branch eXchange (PBX) systems through vendors such as Fonality, Asterisk, Talkswitch, and others, but have not been able to obtain the required internal skill sets or cannot afford the consulting costs to build these virtualized phone systems. With Microsoft Response Point, customers don't have to break the bank and can obtain all the features they need in a phone system out of the box with no license fees. Yes, you heard me right. No license fees. Need to offer long-distance service to your users? No individual license fee charged! Want to receive your voicemail via e-mail? No extra server device or license cost added. This is just the start.

What is Response Point? Response Point can be broken down into software, hardware, and services. The Microsoft CIC team develops the Response Point phone system features and software, partner Original Equipment Manufacturers (OEMs) develop the hardware inclusive of phone system devices, and the Internet Telephony Service Providers (ITSPs) provide the external VoIP calling services.

Let's break this down a bit more.

# Microsoft Response Point Hardware

**Microsoft Response Point** is an OEM solution. Each OEM, currently, Aastra, Quanta, and D-Link, designs the hardware devices for the following universal Response Point hardware components based on Microsoft's OEM design specification (see Figure 3.1):

n **Base Unit device**. This device provides the phone features that run the entire Response Point system. The software running on the Base Unit device includes the phone system feature software created by Microsoft and firmware developed by the OEMs. All OEM phone devices connect to the Base Unit device through the network using a Session Initiation Protocol (SIP) connection, and all Response Point devices are auto-discoverable.

n **Phone devices**. OEM Response Point phone devices, which are also all auto-discoverable on the network, provide the ability to place calls, place callers on hold, park calls, transfer calls, and conference in callers. Each OEM is free to differentiate its Response Point device with additional features. Each Response Point OEM phone device also has a blue colored Response Point button that enables the phone to connect directly to the Base Unit device and initiates the speech recognition feature of the Response Point system. The end user, without any required voice training, can speak into the phone handset or through the speaker phone, which is a high duplex speaker phone to place calls, transfer calls, go to voicemail, and more! This is one of the most highly innovative features of the Response Point system. And what's cool about that? You don't have to remember key codes for actions such as transferring calls, and it's included out of the box, no license fee for this awesome feature!

n **ATA devices**. ATAs are actually common and have been around for decades. An ATA device provides the ability to connect a traditional analog phone line to a digital connection. For Response Point, this means the OEM systems support both Analog and VoIP voice services so that the Response Point customers can choose which services they use for external voice connectivity. Aastra and D-Link have developed separate ATA devices for their Response Point systems, whereas Syspine, as stated before, has its ATA adapters built into the back of its Base Unit device, all of which are also auto-discoverable.

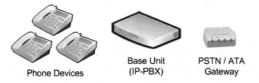

Phone Devices    Base Unit (IP-PBX)    PSTN / ATA Gateway

**FIGURE 3.1** Microsoft Response Point hardware components

As mentioned previously, each OEM Response Point system differs not in its core Response Point features, but in the specific hardware-based features that each OEM adds independently. Let's take a look at each OEM Response Point system and show the differences between each to give you an idea.

## D-Link VoiceCenter

**FIGURE 3.2** D-Link VoiceCenter

I have been working with the Microsoft Communications Innovation Center since the beginning designs of the Response Point product—then known by its code name "Edinburgh"—but I can't tell you how happy I was when I received my first Response Point finalized design device by D-Link. I had been working with this rack-like prototype with a block phone for around three to four months, and here, right in front of me, still secret, was this cool phone system. There is something to be said about seeing a design through its prototype into production. That was the case in this matter. D-Link, one of the world's largest networking device manufacturers, offers a Response Point system through its VoiceCenter product suite (Figure 3.2) including the following components:

n **DVX-2000MS**. This is D-Link's Response Point Base Unit device that includes a push-on start button, audio out/in ports, and capped VGA, mouse, and keyboard ports that were once used to troubleshoot the system and then disabled later. The DVX-2000MS has three indicator lights on the front of the device to display to the user if the device is connected, on, as well as if the device has any errors. This Base Unit device is the smallest of the Response Point OEM vendors in that it has a small, thin, sleek design that stands vertically. Like the other D-Link VoiceCenter Response Point products, this Base Unit is painted black with a silver finish with the D-Link logo (see Figure 3.3).

**FIGURE 3.3** DVX-2000MS

n **DVG-3104MS**. The PSTN/Analog gateway component of the VoiceCenter suite, the D-Link VoiceCenter Gateway provides analog or PSTN support through a series of four included Foreign eXchange Office (FXO) ports. Basically, this means that you can plug four of your existing analog phone lines into the gateway. What's cool about D-Link's and Aastra's approach to the separate ATA adapter is that you can stack additional adapters to support up to 50 analog lines for your Response Point system. Each Gateway also has a Local Area Network (LAN) port to connect your gateway to the local network. Within Response Point Administrator, explained later, you can use the wizard-based software application to add the Gateway to your Response Point infrastructure and config- ure the voice lines directly from the console (see Figure 3.4).

**FIGURE 3.4** DVG-3104MS

n **DPH-125MS**. This phone handset device provides the end user with a Response Point phone that connects through the network to the Base Unit device using auto-discovery. Each Response Point OEM device provides this auto-discovery feature just like the Base Unit and ATA gateway devices. The D-Link phone handset, like all the other OEM Response Point phone handset devices, includes a three-way conferencing button, Dual Tone Multi-Frequency (DTMF) keypad, display screen showing caller-ID and the name of the phone owner plus the extension, date, and time, and a speaker phone button, but more importantly, the blue Response Point but- ton (see Figure 3.5).

**FIGURE 3.5** DPH-125MS

3. SMALL BUSINESS VOICE COMMUNICATIONS WITH MICROSOFT RESPONSE POINT

For more information on D-Link's VoiceCenter product suite, visit its Web site via http://voicecenter.dlink.com.

## Syspine Digital Operator Phone System

**FIGURE 3.6** Syspine Digital Operator Phone System

I'll be honest with you. If I had not read that Quanta was designing the most affordable portable PC device in the world that is part of the One Laptop Per Child (OLPC) project—Google it, and you'll see—I would have never even heard of Quanta. What's surprising to most of the students I have taught is that Quanta is the world's largest notebook PC manufacturer. For the Response Point team, this is great as Quanta has a ton of experience in developing small scale PC products, and to be honest, any VoIP system is really a glorified PC client and server system. Quanta's worldwide success as a manufacturer has given it the confidence to begin making and marketing products under a new brand it created for itself—Syspine—and Response Point is the first product under the new brand. As shown in Figure 3.6, the Syspine Digital Operator Phone System has two separate hardware devices, the Base Unit and phone handset devices, explained as follows:

n **Syspine DOS-A50**. The DOS-A50 is Quanta's Base Unit device that has a built-in ATA gateway and comes in two configurations: one with a four-port ATA adapter and another with an eight-port ATA adapter. The DOS-A50 supports up to eight analog lines internally in the system without the need for a separate ATA adapter. This Base Unit has the same internal features as all the other OEM Base Unit devices, but includes a built-in Dynamic Host Configuration Protocol (DHCP) server as well, which may or not be a benefit as it is turned on by default. For those customers who do not have a DHCP router, this would be a great solution (see Figure 3.7).

**FIGURE 3.7** Syspine DOS-A50

n **Syspine IP-310**. The IP-310 handset comes in two different colors shown in Figures 3.8 and 3.9, white and metallic grey, and includes the same features mentioned previously with the D-Link handset device, with two exceptions. An advanced phone system menu is built into the phone device, and each Syspine handset along with enabled auto-discovery is also Power Over Ethernet (POE) enabled. This means that when you connect an IP-310 to a network that is running a POE switch, the CAT-5 or IP cable that connects the phone to the network then powers the device without the need of the actual power cord, saving you a bit of room and a lot in energy savings!

**FIGURE 3.8** Syspine IP-310 (white)

3. SMALL BUSINESS VOICE COMMUNICATIONS WITH MICROSOFT RESPONSE POINT

**FIGURE 3.9** Syspine IP-310 (metallic grey)

For more information on Quanta's Syspine Response Point phone system, visit its Web site via http://www.syspine.com.

## Aastra AastraLink RP

**FIGURE 3.10** AastraLinkRP

Aastra Telecom, one of the world's largest and Canadian-based telecommunication providers, entered the Response Point market during the Service Pack 1 release. Aastra's entry brought with it a lot of attention to the Response Point system as a market-changing product, as well as a new

Response Point market in Canada, the first international market entry for Response Point. Presented by Yves LaLiberte, Aastra's executive vice president, Response Point has a ton of potential in the small business market in being the most dominant and innovative small business IP phone systems available. Following the launch of Aastra's new Response Point system in July 2008, Aastra demonstrated its new Response Point device suite, which is impressive to say the least. This system makes Response Point look much more mature than the version 1 release with three handset devices plus a mobile Digital Enhanced Cordless Telecommunications (DECT) handset, plus two operator snap-on devices that allow you to see and configure a ton of extensions on the phone handset devices. When I first received my Aastra set of equipment, I knew then that our overall investment had paid off, especially when I was informed that Aastra, unlike any of the other Response Point OEM providers, enables the ability to customize its system solution via a programmable XML interface. This development focus is a link-step into the future of Response Point phone systems as the system moves into more of a hybrid software-integrated phone system with features such as Smart Phones.

As shown in Figure 3.10, Aastra's AastraLink RP system includes the following Response Point devices:

n **AastraLink RP 500 Base Unit**. This Aastra Base Unit device is similar to D-Link and Syspine's Base Unit device in that the device provides all the Response Point phone system features. The RP 500 Base Unit is black and silver trim colored similar to the D-Link set, but is horizontal in design and developed by a telecommunications expert manufacturer (see Figure 3.11).

**FIGURE 3.11** AastraLink RP 500 Base Unit

n **AastraLink RP 540 Gateway**. Similar to the externally provided D-Link VoiceCenter Gateway solution, the Aastra RP 540 Gateway provides up to four FXO ports per gateway device and includes lit status indicators for individual line connectivity (see Figure 3.12).

**FIGURE 3.12** AastraLink RP 540 Gateway

n **6751i RP**. This unique Response Point phone handset provides a
multiline display (up to three lines) and is remnant of executive telecom or PBX phone handsets in the enterprise. Like all of the OEM
Response Point phones, the 675i includes a high duplex speakerphone and is auto-discoverable (see Figure 3.13).

**FIGURE 3.13** 6751i RP

n **6753i RP**. Is similar to the 675i, but supports the AastraLink RP
expansion modules to provide a snap-in device connection to enable
an entire 50 user phone extension operator console (see Figure 3.14).

**FIGURE 3.14** 6753i RP

n **6757i CT RP**. Rounding out the AastraLink RP handset offering, the 6757i CT RP provides support for a connected DECT mobile handset device. Each 6757i CT RP supports up to four connected mobile handsets, and this device sports a beautifully large display with 12 programmable keys as well as support for the provided AastraLink RP expansion modules (see Figure 3.15). This is the Response Point handset of choice at the time of this writing!

**FIGURE 3.15** *6757i CT RP*

n **AastraLink RP expansion modules**. These expansion modules are another innovative solution offering from Aastra with the ability to display up to 50 phone extensions, proving an operator complete visibility into line and extension control (see Figure 3.16).

**FIGURE 3.16** AastraLink RP expansion modules

In summary, Aastra packs a punch with the AastraLink RP system. For more information on Aastra's Response Point products, visit its Web site at http://www.aastra.com.

# Microsoft Response Point Software

Microsoft Response Point software comes in three areas: Base Unit software that runs the phone system features such as the ability to call internally or externally, transfer calls, park calls, and so on. Then there is the administrative and end-user focused software, Microsoft Response Point Administrator and Microsoft Response Point Assistant.

## Microsoft Response Point Base Unit Software

At the heart of the Microsoft Response Point system is the Microsoft Response Point Base Unit software. What most people do not realize is that the entire Response Point system is based on Windows Embedded technology. Inside the Response Point Base Unit device is a 512MB Compact Flash (CF) card that runs a Windows XP Embedded image with configured Response Point software (see Figure 3.17).

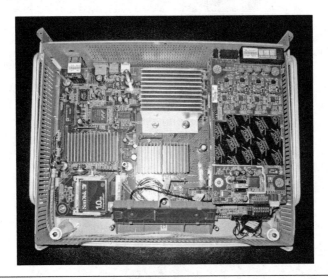

**FIGURE 3.17** Inside of my Syspine Base Unit device; notice the CF card.

What is cool about this architecture is that if I had any problems with the Base Unit stalling or not responding, or if it was just simply corrupt, I could either replace the CF card altogether or just log in to the Base Unit device using a remote data connection from my PC and reinstall the Base

Unit software, even though this is not an officially supported troubleshooting method. The Base Unit software requires a preinstallation of software called the Base Unit Prerequisites software and a speech engine software program. All three programs make up the Response Point Base Unit feature set and enable the Response Point system with all the SIP methods that support the calling speech recognition features that end users enjoy.

Figure 3.18 is a screenshot of the Windows XP Embedded image that provides the Response Point Base Unit services on the Microsoft Response Point Base Unit.

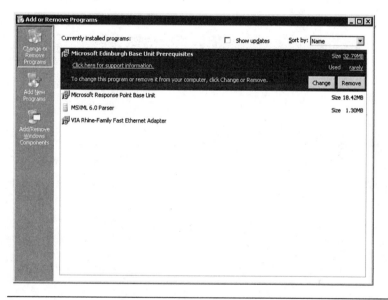

**FIGURE 3.18** Microsoft Response Point Base Unit software

You might be asking, why Windows XP Embedded? Well, the answer has to do with simplicity. Windows XP Embedded is a simple platform to install and create supported OEM drivers for the auxiliary hardware required. Windows Embedded architecture does not allow for malware, spyware, or any virus to intrude into the system as only the three approved software utilities including the system reset, password reset, and diagnostic reporting utilities are allowed to run. That means the customer is provided with a secure platform that cannot be affected by harmful hacking or virus situations that would take down the phone system. This is something none of the Response Point competitors can claim. For more information on Windows Embedded, visit http://www.microsoft.com/windows/embedded.

## Microsoft Response Point Administrator

Included with a purchased set of Microsoft Response Point OEM equipment via a setup CD, Microsoft Response Point Administrator is a software application that allows IT administrators or whoever will be deploying the phone system the ability to do so from one console (see Figure 3.19). This console runs on any Windows operating system and provides a secure connection to the Response Point Base Unit device using Transport Layer Security (TLS) to encrypt the connection between the PC or server being used to control the system and the Base Unit device.

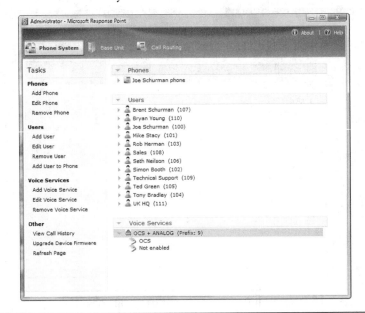

**FIGURE 3.19** Microsoft Response Point Administrator

Response Point Administrator has three system tabs that are universal to any of the Response Point device manufacturers, and a clickable device-specific logo allows administrators to control firmware settings on the devices themselves from the console directly. Very cool! All the operations within the Response Point Administrator console are wizard-based and easy to use. As a test, I let my 12-year-old daughter deploy the Aastra and Syspine system that I have at home. She had no trouble at all!

From the Response Point Administrator console administrators can perform the following tasks:

1. Provision phones.
2. Add users, groups, job locations, and roles.
3. Provision voice services (VoIP and analog).
4. Call History (internal and external calls plus time and type of voice service used).
5. Change Base Unit settings (Date/Time, Password).
6. Configure Unified Messaging (voicemail to e-mail integration).
7. Back up and restore the system.
8. View system diagnostic reports.
9. Upgrade firmware of the Base Unit and phone devices.

That's right! From one console, you can manage an entire 50-phone system.

## Microsoft Response Point Assistant

Included on the same setup CD that Microsoft Response Point Administrator comes with, Microsoft Response Point Assistant is the software application designed for use by end users of the Response Point system. Response Point Assistant provides the ability for users to control all their phone system account settings from a PC application (see Figure 3.20). This is much more convenient than in the past where users of other phone systems had to dial into their voicemail and change their phone account settings through a series of frustrating and time-consuming prompts requiring passwords, key codes, and so on. Microsoft Response Point runs on any Microsoft Windows Operating System and is an auto-start enabled program as well. A user logs in to Response Point Assistant by entering the extension number assigned to him by the phone system and the password he used for voicemail. The default password is **9999**.

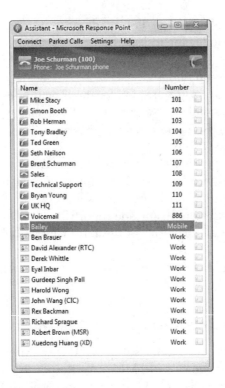

**FIGURE 3.20** Microsoft Response Point Assistant

Once signed in, users can edit a range of settings from changing their voicemail password to changing their voice greeting by uploading .WAV files or recording from the phone. They can add contacts imported from Microsoft Office Outlook or Windows Contacts, set call forwarding and routing properties, Click-to-Call contacts, as well as view the on-hook or off-hook status of other internal Response Point phone users using the topic mentioned previously, SIP Presence. Basically, if another Response Point phone user in the system picks up her phone, the status indicator adjacent to that user's name in the Response Point Assistant User Interface turns red. The user puts the phone back on the cradle, and the color turns to green! Very cool! Just wait until we have a Softphone application out of this!

In Response Point Assistant, Click-to-Call sends a message from the Response Point Assistant software program on the PC through the network to your Response Point phone, and the phone then initiates a speakerphone default enabled call to the contact you selected (see Figure 3.21).

Response Point Assistant is not a Softphone, but is a client or end-user based, personal administration solution for Response Point phone users.

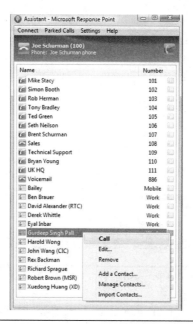

**FIGURE 3.21** Microsoft Response Point Assistant Click-to-Call

Another added benefit of Response Point Assistant is the Call Notification service (see Figure 3.22). Enabled through Response Point Assistant, users can receive onscreen notification alerts showing incoming calls to their phone. Within the Response Point Assistant Settings menu, users can choose whether they want the notification to look in Microsoft Office Outlook or Windows Contacts to add stored contact information to the notification or to just use the default Caller ID for the notification. Either way, Response Point users can see who's calling by looking onscreen. That means a Response Point user could be in a meeting in a conference room and be able to see via laptop all incoming calls going to his desk.

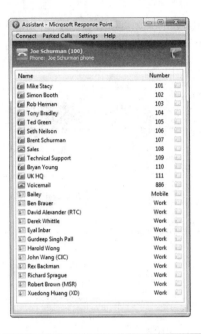

**FIGURE 3.22** Microsoft Response Point Assistant incoming call notification

You can't defer or accept calls within Response Point Assistant as of yet, but still, Response Point Assistant is a cool application that provides a ton of flexibility that allows users of the system to take total control of their phone settings with the click of a mouse.

## Microsoft Response Point Internet Telephony Service Providers

To understand the importance of an ITSP, you have to understand what they offer. As mentioned in Chapter 1, "The Communications Renaissance," ITSPs offer voice communication packages, hosted calling features, and some even provide conferencing services and hosted virtual phone systems. As part of an ITSP's voice communication package, they offer SIP Trunks. A **SIP Trunk** is a connection service provided by an ITSP that connects your IP phone system to the ITSPs hosted service using the Internet Protocol. Today this is used to connect IP phone systems to the Public Switch Telephony Network (PSTN) network.

For Response Point, that means you can configure your Base Unit to connect to the ITSP service, which in turn will connect you to the public telephone network. Response Point also supports analog or PSTN direct communication through the ATA adapters provided by the Response Point OEMs; a physical line connects from a wall jack to one of the ports in the ATAadapter (also known as a PSTN Gateway) providing direct communication to the telephone service provider. The big difference here is that with a SIP Trunk, a digital connection integrates the Response Point Base Unit device to the ITSP through the Internet to the PSTN for outside calling.

Make sense? If not, don't worry. I have traveled the world three times over, visiting almost every Microsoft regional office trying to explain this topic to international audiences. If you can't read me here, do your own homework. First, I recommend that you go to http://www.siptrunk.org and learn more about SIP Trunking than you ever wanted to know. Next, research an ITSP and check out its services offerings. I recommend New Global Telecom (NGT) via http://www.ngt.com. From there you should have a pretty good idea of how this works, and later in this chapter, I'll explain how to configure a SIP Trunk within Response Point and test an outside call using the technology that inspired this entire book, VoIP!

In addition to SIP Trunks, ITSPs also provide Direct Inward Dialing (DID) numbers that go along with the SIP Trunk. DIDs are ordinary phone numbers, but the nice thing is that they can be assigned to a specific extension or user in your office. When outside callers dial a DID number, the call is mapped from the PSTN to the ITSP and then routed to the end of the SIP Trunk, your phone system—in this case, Response Point (see Figure 3.23).

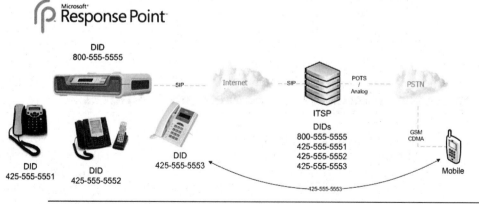

**FIGURE 3.23** Microsoft Response Point ITSP Architecture

Both DID and SIP Trunking services provided by the ITSP are usually provided at a monthly or yearly charge. Some ITSPs also require a contract like you are used to with a wireless provider, but the cool ones don't. Remember that. Some ITSPs also charge a per-DID charge for every DID number you want, and they also provide vanity DIDs like 800 numbers or international numbers that route to your phone system to save the local caller in that region the cost of calling international long distance. Vonage has been pretty popular in providing this service for years.

With the release of Service Pack 1 of Microsoft Response Point, ITSPs suddenly brought a ton of attention to Microsoft. In one way, attention was drawn to Response Point due to the direct SIP Trunking support of the Response Point system, but also as a pre-amp to the future of Microsoft's enterprise Unified Communications solution. SIP Trunking is currently available out of the box with Microsoft Response Point Service Pack 1, and has been finally released as of 2009 with the Unified Communications platform R2 release with Direct SIP support and ITSP integration for SIP Trunking for Microsoft Office Communications Server. If you are reading this book, right now, right here, in this area of the book alone, yep, this part, will be the most critical piece of the pie for the future of voice and unified communications devices, services, and applications in the future. Why? The opportunity. Customers save money, energy, and headache by using SIP services such as SIP Trunking. They have more flexibility in the way that they communicate using SIP through devices, applications, and soon in ways you never thought possible. Partners benefit because not only can they sell and install Microsoft SIP products and services, but they also can sell and install the voice services themselves. ITSPs want to work with Microsoft partners to allow them to offer SIP Trunks and other voice services. Developers benefit because they can create integrated applications that leverage voice services to improve the lives of others in ways not thought possible. Keep a watchful eye and invest wisely in the future of ITSP services!

## Innovative Microsoft Response Point Features

With the July 2008 release of Service Pack 1 for the first version of Microsoft Response Point, many out-of-the-box features might surprise you in regards to a small business phone system. Some of these features were explained earlier in this chapter, but the Response Point Version 1 Service Pack 1 features include the following:

n **Direct SIP Trunking support**. As mentioned earlier, SIP Trunks are provided by the ITSP, and they create a connection from the Response Point Base Unit to the ITSP through the Internet. The ITSP connects to the PSTN to provide incoming and outgoing external calls.

n **DID support**. DIDs are what I like to call "VoIP Digits." Yo, you got my VoIP Digits? Kidding. But seriously, DIDs, as mentioned earlier are real uniformed phone numbers. External callers can call your DID number, and the call is then routed from the PSTN to your phone system via VoIP/SIP through the ITSP. Response Point supports DIDs for the main operator line as well as for individual phone accounts with Version 1, SP1 so that you can scrap your analog or digital phone service provider and truly move to a reliable VoIP platform.

n **Call Status.** Call Status is a fancy word for SIP Presence. The Call Status feature of Microsoft Response Point provides the ability to view another Response Point user's availability. They can visually see the user's Call Status by a change in color in the Response Point Assistant contacts window. If the user's status indicator is red, that means the user is on the phone. If it's green, they are available. Simple as that. Behind the scenes, Call Status is actually invoking a SIP method updating the user's presence in the system based on the user's on-hook/off-hook phone status.

n **Automated virtual attendant**. Using the virtual attendant, even the smallest of companies can look large. Response Point provides a speech-recognition virtual voice-activated attendant so that if you do not have a designated operator you can have the system answer and route calls based on what the caller wants. The virtual attendant can also be configured to answer a preset list of FAQs that the callers might ask such as "What are your hours?" or "What is your fax number?" The speech recognition system running on the Response Point Base Unit device then recognizes these keywords and answers the caller's request. Callers can also use the system to route calls to specific extensions, groups, locations, or job roles.

n **External Access**. Many people overlook this feature, but the External Access feature of Response Point is actually freeing in that you can access all the Response Point phone features you would experience sitting at your desk from a remote phone, especially a mobile phone. Leveraging this feature, you can call into your Response Point account, enter your voicemail password, and then dial out using VoIP or PSTN service. On your mobile phone and need to call internationally?

**3. SMALL BUSINESS VOICE COMMUNICATIONS WITH MICROSOFT RESPONSE POINT**

n **On-Hold music**. This is one of the coolest features from my per-spective in that the services enables the ability to connect a Zune, iPod, or other audio device to a Response Point Base Unit using the Stereo Audio-In port on the back side of the Base Unit.

n **Paging**. Most people don't know this, but from a Microsoft Response Point phone, you can dial 872# and if you connect a speaker or connect the Base Unit to a speaker system or company audio paging system, you can use the phone as your own personal deejay! This simple paging feature requires no configuration except for connecting the stereo out port connect on the back side of the Base Unit device to the speaker system.

n **Interchanging phones**. One cool feature of Microsoft Response Point is that you can purchase a Base Unit device from any of the OEM manufacturers and mix and match any of the OEM phone devices with the Base Unit device. That means you can use a Syspine Base Unit with either or all of the Aastra, D-Link, or Syspine phones.

n **Two-click backup and restore**. I have been working with enter-prise phone systems for more than a decade, and one of the worst-designed solutions in telecommunications hardware and software development is the backup and restore process. Backing up the phone system, including user accounts, call forwarding settings, and so on, is not so bad, but restoring is a nightmare. I once spent more than a week restoring a 15-user phone system, in which only 3 phone users knew how to use the phone. With Microsoft Response Point Administrator, you can back up and restore a system within seconds. The system performs a full backup to file and then you have the choice of restoring options such as a full restore, no voice-mail, and so on. This feature is a time-saver and ingenious.

n **After Hours Receptionist settings.** Ability to specify specific hours and times when incoming calls can be answered by a human recep-tionist and define an after-hours time period when incoming calls can be routed to the built-in Response Point Automated Receptionist.

n **Analog phone support (FXS).** Analog phones can be connected to Response Point through a FXS gateway device that supports the Response Point discovery and provisioning protocol. These devices can then be managed via the Response Point Administrator console.

n **Intercom and paging.** Ability to one-way "Page Dial" specific recipients or "Intercom" a specific recipient via two-way communi-cation by using the Response Point button on an approved OEM-developed handset device or by dialing 0.

- **VPN and multi-subnet support.** Support for remote management and remote office connectivity through a Virtual Private Network (VPN) connection.
- **Incoming call data.** Ability to have the Response Point Assistant application launch a customized URL when a user receives an incoming call. This lets a developer integrate Response Point into another application. Information appended to the URL will include the extension being dialed, the user at that extension, the time, the incoming caller's caller ID, and the name associated with that caller ID. The feature is turned on/off/specified in the registry of the machine running the Response Point Assistant software application.
- **Trunk device support.** Response Point already supports both analog lines and VoIP service through a broadband connection (that is, SIP trunk). Response Point Service Pack 2 adds two other common phone trunk technologies: digital trunks (T1, and so on); and VoIP trunks delivered via an on-premises gateway device that improves quality of service.
- **Parked call return.** Any call that has been parked for three minutes will be automatically returned to the extension that parked it. If there is no answer, the call is directed to the auto-attendant or receptionist.
- **Personal contacts can be called with specific voice services.** When editing a personal contact within the Response Point Assistant software, the user can specify which voice service to be used when voice-dialing or click-to-calling using Analog, ITSP, or Digital Trunk voice services.
- **Escape from voicemail greeting before recording starts.** Ability for a caller to press 0 while listening to a voicemail greeting to be routed back into the system or operator (if enabled).
- **Optional call forwarding prompt.** In some cases, users do not want call forwarding to be announced. Each user is able to specify whether they want their callers to hear an announcement when forwarding calls.
- **Changes to calls from an external access number to a DID number.** Previously, when a call was made from an "external access" number to a DID number, the system let the caller enter her PIN and then forwarded the call to the DID's extension. Unfortunately, there was no way to go to the internal auto- attendant in this scenario. In SP2, this flaw is corrected.
- **In-band DTMF improvements.** DTMF tones, also known as touch-tones, can be either transmitted as audible tones within the audio

stream carrying the voice conversation (in-band) or in a separate channel that is not mixed with the audio stream (out-of-band). Out-of-band is more accurate but not supported by all service providers.

Previously, in-band DTMF was used all the time, in order to maximize interoperability. However, this created some quality issues due to the detection of false-positives. (Tones that naturally occur within speech are occasionally mistakenly assumed by an application to be a DTMF tone.) SP2 uses out-of-band DTMF (the more accurate method) whenever appropriate. SP2 also improves the accuracy of in-band DTMF to improve performance with service providers that do not support out-of-band DTMF.

The following is a full list of Microsoft Response Point Version 1, Service Pack 1 features:

- Call Status (Presence)
- Call history reporting
- New, advanced call handling options for easy transferring, parking, and dialing
- Upgraded firmware on phones and phone line adapters
- SIP Trunking
- DID numbers to better connect your employees and customers via SIP Trunking
- Voice-dial access to free directory assistance
- Improvements to Speech Recognition within phone devices and Built-in Auto-Attendant
- 64-bit compatibility

## Response Point and Small Business Server Integration

Because Microsoft Response Point's target market is small business, it was only natural that Response Point integrate with Microsoft's top small business software platform with Microsoft Windows Small Business Server. Now in its 2008 release, Small Business Server (SBS) packs a punch and offers every tool small business organizations can use to quickly and affordably manage and execute their IT systems and software.

A powerful feature of SBS is simplified management. IT administrators or, in most cases, small business owners, can view from one screen, system events related to their entire SBS environment, which can include their Web site, internal portal, e-mail, and much more. Through a simple add-on solution, called the Microsoft Response Point Status Monitor for Windows Small Business Server, Microsoft added IP phone system manageability to the Windows Small Business Server reporting service only further differentiating Microsoft Small Business Server and Microsoft Response Point from other competitive small business solutions in the marketplace. Now that's innovation and let me also mention that this integration service is free!

How does the Response Point Status Monitor software work? Easy. An administrator or end user, because this is so easy, downloads the Status Monitor software online via http://www.microsoft.com/downloads and searches for "Response Point Status Monitor." Once downloaded, the software is installed on the server running SBS. After running the setup.exe file on the SBS server, a simple configuration menu allows the user to specify the Microsoft Response Point system she wants to manage via an autodiscoverable drop-down box that shows the Microsoft Response Point system currently running inside the network.

Figure 3.24 depicts the Response Point Status Monitor login screen for Windows Small Business Server.

**FIGURE 3.24** Microsoft Response Point Status Monitor for Windows Small Business Server login

From there, that's it! The system automatically sends events from the Microsoft Response Point system directly to the Windows Small Business Server system. This enables administrators or end users to not only view system events from the SBS reports, but also receive e-mail alerts or SMS text alerts on their mobile devices as well, ensuring that their business system is up and running at all times and limiting those unforeseen surprises.

# The Gateway to Voice and Unified Communications

As you learn in Chapter 4, "Enterprise Voice with Microsoft Unified Communications," IP gateways play a large role in voice and unified communications products across small business and enterprise markets for every competitor. These gateways provide the unique ability for companies to integrate data with traditional telephony services including fax services, enabling a truly well-rounded converged telephony solution.

There are many players in the voice and unified communications gateway market, but the most popular and most known third-party gateway manufacturers (excluding the big boys such as Nortel and Cisco) include companies such as Quintum, AudioCodes, and Dialogic. There are many others, but these three play a large role in integrating voice services for Microsoft.

In fall 2008, Quintum announced two gateway solutions at the IT Expo event in California that now provide the ability to integrate Microsoft Response Point to T1, E1, PRI, Fax, and analog voice services through their Quintum Response Point Analog Gateway and their Quintum Response Point T1/E1/PRI Gateway as showcased in the next section.

## Quintum Response Point Gateways

The following information is a direct excerpt from Quintum's Response Point Gateway microsite via http://www.quintum.com/responsepoint:

> Quintum offers two gateway products for the Response Point Phone System: an analog 4-port FXS gateway and a digital T1/E1/PRI gateway.
>
> ### Quintum Response Point Analog Gateway
>
> The Quintum Response Point analog 4-Port FXS Gateway supports up to four simultaneous VoIP calls and lets you connect your Response Point phone system with your existing analog phones, fax machines, and other modem-based devices (see Figure 3.25).

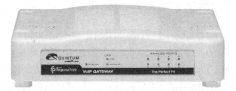

FIGURE **3.25** Quintum Response Point Analog Gateway

### Quintum Response Point T1/E1/PRI Gateway

The Quintum Response Point digital T1/E1/PRI Gateway supports T1, E1, or PRI connections (see Figure 3.26). These digital gateways support up to 30 simultaneous VoIP calls and are capable of interfacing with a full E1. This flexibility makes these gateways the perfect fit for small and medium businesses with digital telephone network connections.

**FIGURE 3.26** Quintum Response Point T1/E1/PRI Gateway

# Evangelyze Communications SmartVoIP

In addition to the NET Quintum gateway offerings announced at IT Expo 2008, Quintum and my organization, Evangelyze Communications, have created a direct integration between Microsoft's Unified Communications platform and Microsoft Response Point to create the first ever, fully integrated, Microsoft voice solution.

Launched at the VoiceCon 2008 conference in San Francisco on November 12, 2008, our organization in collaboration with NET Quintum showcased the ability to connect Microsoft Office Communications Server with Microsoft Response Point to enable direct SIP communication between both product platforms (see Figure 3.27). The purpose of this solution is to provide organizations with remote office locations the ability to communicate, eliminating long-distance charges between locations and using a holistic Microsoft Voice and Unified Communications solution. Further details on this release can be found on our Web site via http://www.evangelyze.net.

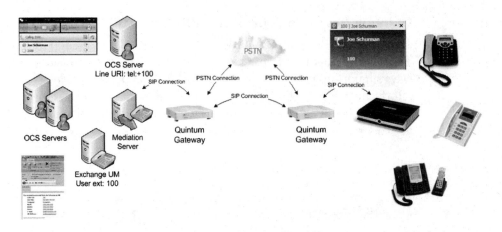

**FIGURE 3.27** The Evangelyze Communications SmartVoIP architecture

As you can see, through these gateway solutions, there are endless integration possibilities to connect remote offices on a global scale bypassing the public telephone network and lowering an organization's Total Cost of Ownership (TCO) by offering devices and integration services at a fraction of Microsoft's competitor's costs.

# Experiencing Voice with Microsoft Response Point

You've read the hype, now let's experience Response Point firsthand. Follow these steps to use the most innovative phone system for small businesses.

## Step 1—Purchase a Response Point System

Finding a Response Point system is easy today, leveraging the Microsoft Response Point Value Added Reseller (VAR) network made available via the Microsoft Response Point Web site at http://www.microsoft.com/responsepoint. Through each VAR, you can purchase equipment and services to install your Response Point system quickly and painlessly. In addition to the Response Point VAR network, one of the announcements made this year from the Response Point team included the sale of Syspine Response Point systems online through Costco.com. Now, you can purchase an entire Response Point system or phone handset devices over the phone or via the Web through the most price efficient commercial and consumer shopping site in the world. But, to get a taste of what Response

Point can offer, you can purchase a demo kit from Evangelyze Communications, my company. We have developed an entire kit that includes a Base Unit, three phones, a Kyocera KR2 Mobile Broadband router, surge protector, all the power and Ethernet cables you need, and the software CD out of the box. To purchase, visit http://www.evangelyze.net/products.asp. The full kit costs $2,599 USD inclusive of a rolling, travel case with custom foam inserts for the devices. Otherwise, a demo kit, with shipping costs $1,200 through us and around $1,000 directly from the OEM. Costco.com does not offer a demo kit price.

## Step 2—Configure Microsoft Response Point Hardware

After you have purchased your Response Point hardware from the OEMs (Quanta/Syspine, Aastra, or D-Link) or a bundled kit from Evangelyze Communications, the next step in this model is to configure your hardware. To begin your Microsoft Response Point hardware configuration use the following steps:

1. Provide enough space to lay out the provided OEM Response Hardware including the Base Unit, three phones, ATA adapter (if not built-in), router, and cabling.
2. Connect all devices to a router that supports DHCP using the provided Ethernet cables.
3. Connect all devices to a power source and make sure that the surge protector is turned off. A surge protector is recommended.

---

**NOTE** If your POE phone devices are connected to a POE router/switch, you do not have to connect a power source to the phone devices.

---

4. After the network and power cables are connected, turn on the surge protector. At this point all devices will turn on and an IP address is automatically obtained from the DHCP router or server.
5. Connect a PC to the router that is connected to your Response Point devices so that it can obtain an IP address as well. You can connect your PC directly to the router if a port is available, or you can connect your PC to one of the Response Point phone devices using the 10/100MB switch located on the back side of the phone device as depicted in Figure 3.28.

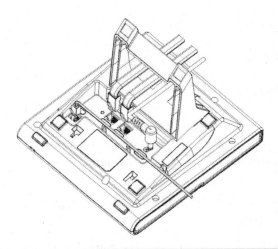

**FIGURE 3.28** Example of Syspine IP phone with dual-port switch

## Step 3—Configure Response Point Software

Now that the devices are connected and powered, we will install and configure the Microsoft Response Point software that is required to administrate the deployment of the entire Response Point system through Microsoft Response Point Administrator and to provide end users with the ability to leverage intuitive account features through Microsoft Response Point Assistant.

1. After your PC is connected to this network, install Response Point Administrator and Response Point Assistant software via the provided CD or download directly from http://www.microsoft.com/downloads—search for "Response Point."

2. Follow the installation wizard to install both Response Point Assistant and Administrator on the PC and then run Response Point Administrator by either clicking on the provided startup icon/desktop shortcut created during the setup process or from the Start menu by choosing Start, All Programs, Microsoft Response Point Administrator.

3. After Response Point Administrator opens, your Response Point Base Unit device should auto-provision itself so that your application can see it in the Base Unit list.

4. When you see your listed Base Unit device, double-click on the listing or select the listed Base Unit and click on the Connect button (see Figure 3.29).

**FIGURE 3.29** Microsoft Response Point Administrator login

5. You then are presented with a password entry form. Type in the default password, **admin**.
6. After your password has been entered, you are able to configure your Response Point system using Response Point Administrator.

## Step 4—Configuring Phones, Users, and Features

Now we add users and phones to the system. Similar to how the Base Unit was located via auto-provisioning, so are the phone devices and the ATA adapters.

1. To add a phone, make sure to select the Phone System tab within the Response Point Administrator console. In the left-hand corner under Tasks, click on the Add Phone task.
2. When the Add Phone menu appears, check the check box that states that the phone is connected and has power (see Figure 3.30).

**FIGURE 3.30** Adding the phone wizard

3. In the list of available phones, choose one of the phone devices and click Next (see Figure 3.31).

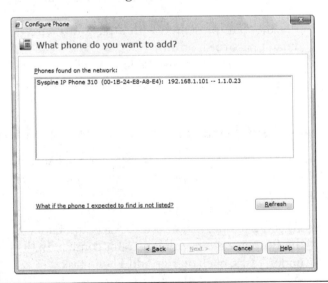

**FIGURE 3.31** Phone auto-provision list

4. Now, you assign a user, group, job location, or role to the phone device in one of the phone assignment fields (see Figure 3.32). Each OEM provides phone devices that support a different amount of assignments/lines. For example, some Aastra phone devices support six and nine lines per phone, whereas D-Link and Syspine only support four assignments. During the assignment section of the wizard, click on the Add New User button.

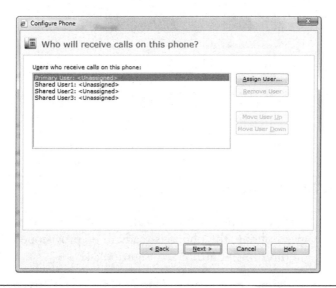

**FIGURE 3.32** Phone user assignment

5. Fill out the new user information menu and either create a user, group, job location, or role by configuring the account type drop-down section of the screen. After filling out the name information, click OK (see Figure 3.33).

**FIGURE 3.33** User/Account properties

6. After the users, groups, locations, and/or roles are selected for a given phone, the phone is ready to be provisioned. Now, just click on the Finish button (see Figure 3.34).

**FIGURE 3.34** Name of phone

7. Verify that the phone has been successfully provisioned, and then click Close to exit the wizard (see Figure 3.35).

**FIGURE 3.35** Completing the phone provisioning process

8. Repeat this process for the other two or more phone devices you want to use and note that you can create Response Point accounts separately from adding a device by using the Add User task.

9. After accounts are created, open the Response Point Assistant application to log in to the system as one of these users using the extension number and by entering the default password, **9999** (see Figure 3.36). You then see a list of accounts in the system.

**FIGURE 3.36** Microsoft Response Point Assistant

## Step 5—Testing Response Point Features

Now that we have added phones and devices, let's test some of the calling features of Response Point. First, let's place a call using voice dialing. To do this, use the following instructions:

1. Use the Assistant to log in to one of your phones. Now, dial into that phone from another extension: Just press the "Magic Blue Button" Response Point button on the phone (see Figure 3.37). The speaker will now initiate and call the speech recognition system.

**FIGURE 3.37** Response Point "Magic Blue Button"

2. Say the name or group of the extension you are logged in to Response Point Assistant with. The phone then automatically dials the extension you requested.
3. Notice that on your PC you now have an onscreen notification of the incoming call through Response Point Assistant (see Figure 3.38). Pick up the handset of the other device to answer the call.
4. Now we will park and transfer a call. From the extension/phone you received the call on and are logged in to Response Point Assistant with, click on the "Magic Blue Button" again. This parks the call. Hang up the handset a second after clicking the button. Now the call is parked.
5. From within Response Point Assistant on your PC, you can now look under the Parked Calls menu and notice your parked call in the list (see Figure 3.39). From Response Point Assistant under the Parked Call menu, click on the parked call. This sends the parked call to your phone.

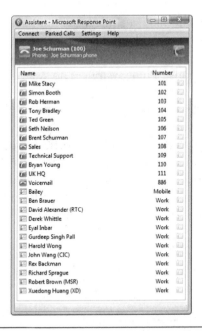

**FIGURE 3.38** Response Point Assistant incoming call notification

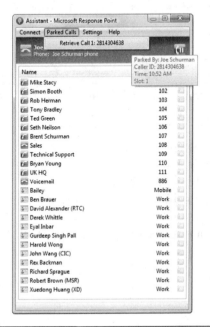

**FIGURE 3.39** Response Point Assistant Parked Call List

6. Pick up the handset on this phone again. Now, press the "Magic Blue Button" and say "Transfer my call to" and say the name or extension of the other phone that is not in use, but provisioned in the Response Point system. The system now voice routes/transfers your call to the other extension.

7. Now let's try outside line connectivity using VoIP. To add VoIP service, you have to contact and purchase a VoIP service plan from one of the Response Point certified voice partners such as NGT, CBeyond, and Junction Networks currently. After you sign up for your voice service through these providers, within Response Point Administrator on the left-hand side under Voice Services on the Phone System tab, click on Add Voice Service (see Figure 3.40).

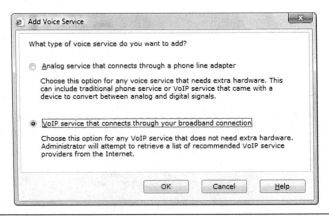

**FIGURE 3.40** Response Point Administrator adding ITSP Voice Services

8. The Add Voice Service Wizard now initiates. Choose VoIP in the option box provided and click Next.

9. Now select your VoIP provider out of the provided drop-down arrow (see Figure 3.41).

10. Fill out the information listed onscreen provided by your VoIP service provider including the Address of Record (AOR), passwords, and other information (see Figure 3.42). When finished, click Next.

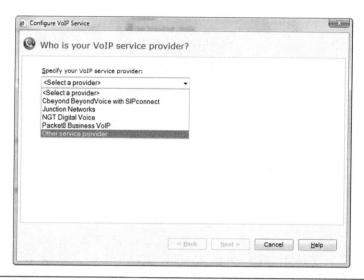

**FIGURE 3.41** Response Point Administrator ITSP Service Provider List

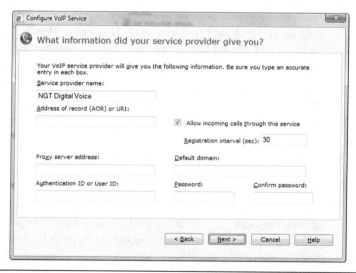

**FIGURE 3.42** Response Point Administrator ITSP Service Provider Account Information

11. Now, you can assign Direct Inward Dialing numbers to your main Base Unit built-in Auto-Attendant or Operator as well as assign DIDs to specific users within the system (see Figure 3.43). When finished, click Finish. The system now provisions your VoIP service.

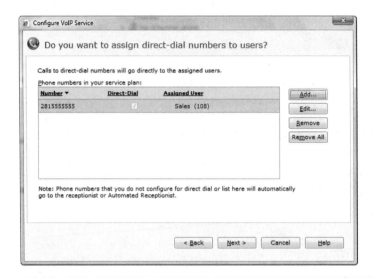

**FIGURE 3.43** Response Point Administrator ITSP Provider DID Configuration

12. To test outside dialing via voice, you need to call an outside contact either created or imported into Response Point Assistant using Microsoft Office Outlook or Windows Contacts. Let's add a contact by importing one from Microsoft Office Outlook. To do so, open Response Point Assistant and choose Contacts from the Settings menu.

13. Choose the drop-down selection in the Import from field (see Figure 3.44).

14. Import one of your contacts that has a number outside the existing Response Point directory. You can create a contact within Outlook if you don't have one. Click OK when finished.

15. Notice that adjacent to the imported contact there is a Bypass Auto-Attendant check box (see Figure 3.45). This is used so that if you have a contact that you want to have call directly into your extension without calling the Response Point built-in Auto-Attendant or physically assigned Operator first, you can.

16. Now from the Response Point phone that shares the same extension you have logged in to with using Response Point Assistant, click on the "Magic Blue Button" and say "Call [NAME OF YOUR CONTACT]." The system now places an outside call using your VoIP service to this contact.

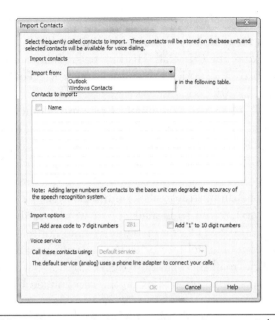

**FIGURE 3.44** Response Point Assistant Contact Resource Selection

**FIGURE 3.45** Response Point Assistant Importing Outlook Contacts

17. You can check the call record of that communication within Response Point Administrator on the Phone System tab as well by clicking on the Call History task. Take a look at the provided records and notice the call you made via VoIP to the outside contact. Pretty cool, eh?

18. Now let's test voicemail. Response Point has built-in Unified Messaging in the form of voicemail to e-mail functionality. There are two steps to configure Unified Messaging within Response Point. The first is to configure the e-mail server connection within Response Point Administrator. Within the Base Unit tab of Response Point Administrator, click on the Configure E-mail Server task.

19. In the Configure E-mail Server window, fill in the provided fields with the SMTP server name, e-mail address you will use to send voicemail attachments, as well as your username and password. If your e-mail server requires SSL connectivity, make sure to choose the provided check box on the screen (see Figure 3.46).

**FIGURE 3.46** Response Point Administrator Base Unit E-mail Settings (Voicemail to E-mail)

20. Now, in Response Point Assistant, under the Settings menu, choose Voicemail. Specify that you want to receive voicemail attachments via e-mail and then type in the e-mail address or e-mail addresses separated by semicolons to where you want to receive the actual voicemail attachments (see Figure 3.47).

21. Either by asking your outside contact or just by calling your extension using one of the other Response Point phones, call your extension that you have been connected to using Response Point Assistant. At this time, do not answer the call, but let the call go directly to voicemail.

**FIGURE 3.47** Response Point Assistant User E-mail Settings

22. You can review your voicemail directly from the phone itself using the voicemail button on the phone, but now let's check the voicemail via your e-mail inbox on your PC within Microsoft Office Outlook or whatever e-mail program you use. You should notice an unread e-mail message with an attachment in your inbox. If you don't, check the Event Log within Response Point Administrator to see whether there was a problem connecting to your e-mail server, or check your Junk E-mail box to see whether the message was stuck there (see Figure 3.48).

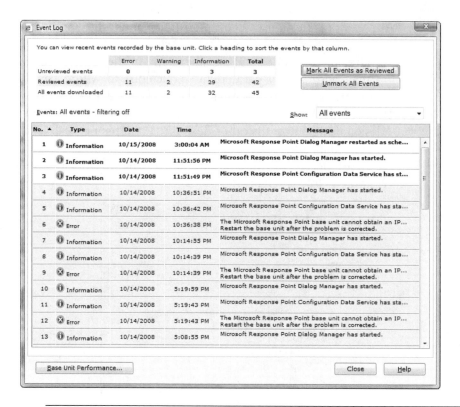

**FIGURE 3.48** Response Point Administrator Call History Report

23. When the message is sent successfully, you receive an e-mail message in your inbox on your PC, Mac, browser, or mobile device (see Figure 3.49). When you open the message, open the voicemail attachment and simply listen to your new voicemail.

24. Also, you can view your Response Point voicemail e-mails on your mobile device as well. Very cool if you are on the road and have a device that accepts e-mails and attachments. Figure 3.50 depicts a Response Point voicemail received on an iPhone.

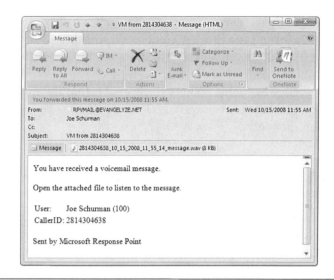

**FIGURE 3.49** Microsoft Office Outlook E-mail with Response Point Voicemail Message

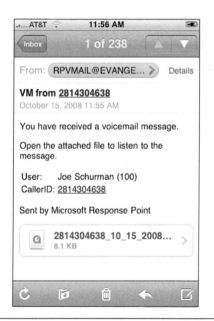

**FIGURE 3.50** iPhone E-mail with Response Point Voicemail Message

You can then listen to your voicemail without having to dial anything!

This is just a taste of what you can do with Microsoft Response Point, but understand the value here. All Microsoft Response Point's competitors offer similar solutions at twice or even triple the price, and their features are not as easy to enable. What's really cool is that the instructions listed in this chapter will take you around 20 minutes or less to complete if you follow them diligently.

## My Personal Response Point Response

Since this is my book, I will be honest with you so that this book sounds a little less like a marketing brochure and more like a guide. In respect to the three OEM Response Point vendors, are all equal in what they offer in a Response Point phone system regarding system features, because the Base Unit software is the same. But I would rank each as shown in Table 3.1, based on the Response Point marketing pillars as a matrix.

**Table 3.1** Grading Response Point OEMs

| OEM | Easy to Use | Easy to Manage | Easy to Grow |
|---|---|---|---|
| D-Link VoiceCenter | X | | |
| Syspine DOS | | X | |
| AastraLink RP | | | X |

I like the simplicity of D-Link's VoiceCenter design, but the system's appearance is a bit immature for a professional-looking phone system. This is a system that would be better fit for a home office implementation with maybe one or two phones and could be purchased from a local Best Buy or other electronics store.

Quanta/Syspine's Response Point system was my system of choice before Aastra came to town. I liked the executive design of the Syspine phones and the simplicity of including the PSTN Gateway/ATA adapter as part of the Base Unit build. However, I did not like the included ATA adapter in that if the adapter has problems, you have to send the entire Base Unit in for repair. I also was not fond of the DHCP server being turned on automatically in the earlier shipments of this product, but I did see the value of it being included for small businesses that do not have a DHCP server, do not have a router, or simply want to consolidate services.

I also love and respect the Syspine team. These are the easiest people in the world to work with, and I have never met a kinder person than Sam Liu at Quanta.

Aastra, the new kid on the block, also brings the cool toys to the playground. I have not stress tested the system enough to find any problems, and I like their focus on the multiline extension phones, the mobile handset solution, but more importantly the XML capabilities of the phone devices. As I mentioned earlier in this book, the future of voice and unified communications will be in how software will transform voice services. This is definitely the case with Aastra's devices in that I can provide business applications to these phone devices that improve an organization's business processes. For example, we are actually able to provide a branch office solution with Aastra's AastraLinkRP solution through our Evangelyze Communications SmartVoIP solution. I can query the Microsoft Active Director contact information store and push these corporate contacts, via an online XML-based web service to remote offices that have deployed AastraLinkRP phones, straight to the phone device. This provides a shared directory of contacts throughout an enterprise organization running Microsoft Office Communications Server with remote offices running Microsoft Response Point devices. I believe Aastra's AastraLink RP system will definitely mature the overall product line for the Microsoft Response Point business group and raise the bar for future device manufacturers on the next OEM list. Aastra is also well versed in Unified Communications technology as it is currently the #1 Telco provider in Europe, and I see it playing an integral part of the future of UC and branch office technology for Microsoft. Additionally, my family is from Canada so I have a soft spot for Canadian-based companies!

## Microsoft's Internal Perception of Microsoft Response Point

In regards to how Response Point is viewed from within Microsoft as well as through Microsoft partners, there are many mixed views. Coming from the enterprise Unified Communications market, many internal Microsoft representatives laughed at the initial product release and viewed Response Point as a wannabe Unified Communications solution. They did not take the time to realize that Response Point addresses a different market segment to help small businesses as well as provides a voice solution that does not require four to five servers at a minimum and more than $100,000 in services, hardware, and software licenses. For less than $10,000 you can have a 50 IP phone Response Point system, which includes innovative voice features without charging a customer a single software license fee. My response to internal Microsoft employees and partners who have been hesitant to adopt Response Point is to not be ignorant and to understand what the solution provides. Response Point is a pet project of Bill Gates himself, and this team and solution offering has delivered high-quality VoIP and IP phone services at a price that is affordable to small businesses and branch offices in the future. From a Microsoft Response Point marketing perspective, the product speaks to the marketing pillars that have been set forth in that the product is easy to manage, easy to use, and easy to grow. Through the power of software, we are able to provide integration services such as the Evangelyze Communications SmartVoIP solution, further extending the Microsoft voice platform in ways not thought possible, and bottom line, building the credibility of Microsoft in the telecommunications industry.

# CHAPTER 4

# ENTERPRISE VOICE WITH MICROSOFT UNIFIED COMMUNICATIONS

Now, we will cover voice in the enterprise, which has been a fluctuating and quickly evolving market over the past century. Through this experience, you will learn how a software manufacturer like Microsoft has transformed the telephony industry through software-powered voice and will forever change existing voice communications as you know and use them today with the Microsoft Unified Communications platform.

In a market that has been dominated by the likes of Cisco, Nortel, Avaya, Aastra, Siemens, NEC, and other large telecommunications manufacturers as well as hybrid IP-PBX system providers such as Digium (Switchvox), and Fonality, Microsoft, the software manufacturer, not telephony device manufacturer, has made an enormous splash that is transforming the unified communications industry forever through the power of software and has played a strategic role to now be considered a leader in the Unified Communications market as identified by Gartner Research within its Magic Quadrant for Unified Communications, as shown in Figure 4.1.

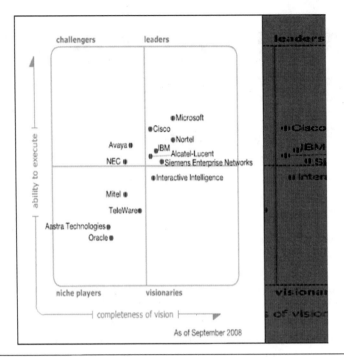

**FIGURE 4.1** Magic Quadrant for Unified Communications

Gartner UC Magic Quadrant (© 2008 Gartner Research)

Originally targeting mail, collaboration, and Instant Messaging (IM) separately, Microsoft has now combined the Office suite of products—Outlook, Word, Excel, and PowerPoint—with the MVPs of Microsoft enterprise products, Microsoft Exchange Server and Microsoft Office SharePoint Server to compete in a mature marketplace from both an application and device perspective. I have been personally involved with Microsoft's independent UC products since Microsoft Exchange 5.5 and Live Communications Server 2003. Beginning with IM, Microsoft targeted products including IBM's popular Sametime Instant Messaging server. I actually left IBM Global Services to begin working on the first Live Communications Server deployment at a multibillion dollar oil, gas, and exploration company headquartered in London, England, to enable this conglomerate with a new IM solution to compete with their internal IBM Sametime solution. Following this project, I helped organize the largest IM deployment for a financial institution and then a U.S. federal agency, all existing IBM Sametime customers. Needless to say, IBM became threatened by this new kid on the block—not me, Microsoft—and began to offer Sametime licenses for free.

After three releases of Live Communications Server (2003, 2005, and 2005 SP1), the Unified Communications team decided to focus on integrating voice into the collaborative mix and changed the name of the product to **Office Communications Server (OCS)**. Now in its 2007 R2 release, OCS packs a punch by providing enterprise, secure IM, but also enterprise voice and conferencing solutions including recording and archiving tools. Adding integration with Microsoft's signature enterprise messaging system, Microsoft Exchange Server, the Unified Communications solution provides integrated Unified Messaging as well as the ability to dial into Exchange Server via phone to retrieve e-mail and voicemail messages and to create and edit meetings and conferences all via phone.

The OCS client, Office Communicator, is now an all-in-one client to enable Instant Messaging between internal and partner organizations as well as with the public networks including AOL, Yahoo, and MSN/Windows Live. Communicator also is to be used as a VoIP and Remote Call Control (RCC) client to communicate via voice from your PC to internal and external system users. With built-in conferencing solutions that can be hosted internally within the OCS with Live Meeting 2007, users can host conferences as well as create conferences and meetings directly from within Outlook or Communicator making collaborating and communicating with contacts easy. Adding Microsoft Office SharePoint Server to the mix, users can enable Instant Messaging, conferencing, and voice directly from within portal sites, rounding out a truly collaborative, communications-enabled solution.

How does the market perceive this? Well, if this is the first time you have read anything about Microsoft's Unified Communications platform, it may be as confusing to you as it is to market analysts. Still, Microsoft is viewed as a leader in this market area and will be the most dominating market share leader starting with the Wave 14 release of the product, which includes all the SIP/VoIP calling features without the need of gateways or in-between server routing solutions that drive up cost and complexity of a deployment. Cisco and Nortel, two dominating PBX and Unified Communications providers, have maintained market share only because their solutions are based on the proven and legacy focus on hardware devices. The two organizations work against each other in cross-competitive marketing campaigns that reflect whose hardware is cheaper or better as of now, and I was a large part of this with my marketing release of the Nortel UC Green story, whose hardware is more energy efficient. Microsoft partners with these organizations currently with a sugar-coated marketing campaign of not to "Rip & Replace" your hardware, but

"Surround the Socket" by using the vendor's hardware and Microsoft's software connecting users to phone devices and services using Microsoft OCS and Microsoft Office Communicator. For some reason, Cisco, Nortel, and others bought into this, or more than likely, were paid to participate in this campaign, hopefully knowing full well that Microsoft will directly compete with all these leading Telco providers head on by 2010. Whoever missed this is either extremely naive or too hesitant to communicate concern. Regardless, this is where we are: transitioning as a market and from a technology perspective of hardware-based communication solutions to software-powered voice solutions.

Now that you somewhat understand where the current market lies, let's dive into what products make up the Microsoft Unified Communications platform.

# Microsoft Office Communications Server

Office Communications Server (OCS) is Microsoft's enterprise voice server, the cornerstone of the Microsoft Unified Communications platform, and the future of Microsoft's Voice and Unified Communications vision. This software-powered voice solution will be the market leading and market-changing voice platform server of the century. OCS has gone through many version releases and upgrades—some good, some shocking—but all necessary to prepare the product for its sole purpose in the industry, the ultimate PBX killer. Forget the "VoIP as you are" campaign hailed highly from Microsoft today. In the next two years, Microsoft OCS will be the socket and will enable branch offices and enterprise organizations to leverage a price performance voice solution that spans applications, networks, and devices, reminding me of Bill Gates' initial vision around the .NET strategy of connecting people, applications, and devices across ubiquitous networks. This is it folks, the real deal.

## From RTC to UC

Before OCS was part of the Unified Communications Business Group at Microsoft, its predecessor, LCS, was part of the Real-time Collaboration (RTC) Business Group. Back "in the day" things were much simpler. We didn't have to worry about voice channels, Quality of Service (QoS) issues, and so on, and could just focus on the collaboration functionality of this newly released SIP server from Microsoft. Back then, we just worried about server placement and federation with public IM networks such as Yahoo, MSN, and AOL, which were the source of the biggest headaches—security and archiving. I can't remember how many hundreds of internal Microsoft employees and field reps in each region of the world I trained just on what Transport Layer Security was. Having worked on some of the largest and initial RTC projects and receiving one of the first two Microsoft Most Valuable Professionals awards within the RTC community, I witnessed the evolution of LCS to OCS through the addition and focus on integrated voice services through VoIP and traditional telephony solutions through the PBX. At that time, our incubation center group grew into an actual Business Group (BG) at Microsoft with the internal merger of the RTC team and the prestigious and money making Microsoft Exchange Server team. Two years later, the BG is now composed of some of the top voice communications talent from a sales, marketing, and product development perspective in the industry. Bottom line, it was a challenging transition, but we all made it through and are all now poised to make a killing in the market.

## Office Communications Server Editions

Many people think that OCS is simply just another Microsoft server. They do not realize that there are many components to the OCS environment, including the Multi-Point Control Units (MCUs) that are used within a single or multi-OCS server configuration to host voice, conferencing, and data (Instant Messaging, Presence, and so on) as well as archiving, call recording, PBX Remote Call Control, monitoring servers, mediation gateways, and not to exclude, conferencing, phone devices, and a full-featured end-user client application in Office Communicator. To provide you with a better understanding of these components, I'll break these down one by one.

### OCS Multipoint Control Units

Let me start by stating that OCS is a SIP and RTP server. As mentioned earlier, SIP clients, which would be the users of the OCS client application, Office Communicator, connect to this SIP/RTP server to consume features such as voice, video, conferencing, and Instant Messaging. In a SIP/RTP environment, features, such as audio, video, voice, Web conferencing, and Instant Messaging, are provided and hosted through an MCU. With the Microsoft Unified Communications platform there are three MCUs—one each for Audio/Video, Instant Messaging, and Web Conferencing (see Figure 4.2).

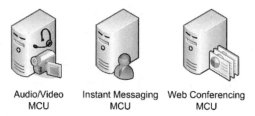

Audio/Video        Instant Messaging    Web Conferencing
MCU                MCU                  MCU

**FIGURE 4.2** Microsoft Unified Communications platform

These MCUs can host a certain number of users to provide the Unified Communications features that the end users consume to communicate and collaborate with internal and external contacts. Because the MCUs can only handle a certain number of users (based on hardware and usage patterns), OCS is broken out into two separate editions, Enterprise and Standard.

### Audio/Video MCU

The OCS Audio/Video MCU provides the ability to host audio and video sessions within a Unified Communications environment. End users leveraging the Microsoft OCS client, Microsoft Office Communicator, can participate in voice and video sessions with other contacts inside the corporate network as well as remotely and with external participants. The Audio/Video MCU enables this capability by hosting this traffic and enabling the required audio and video codecs to perform the transmission of these SIP packages across the network. In the R2 release of Microsoft OCS 2007, the Audio/Video MCU plays a very important role by enabling HD-quality video communications so that you can truly use video conferences on a wider scale and video conversations for a small group or 1:1 format. You can feel as if you are right there with the party on the other end of the camera!

### Instant Messaging MCU

The OCS Instant Messaging MCU is dedicated to host the IM services used by the OCS client application, Office Communicator. Through the IM MCU, Communicator sends and receives Instant Messages throughout the internal OCS environment as well as brokers IM communications between the internal environment with federated/connected OCS environments and public IM networks such as AOL, Yahoo, and Windows Live/MSN. As explained earlier, Microsoft uses SIP as its communication protocol for video, voice, and data. Through the MCU architecture, the

IM MCU provides the ability to enable IM data as well as presence. This technology is not really anything new as Microsoft has used SIP as its default protocol for IM through previous Unified Communications product versions with Live Communications Server 2003—Live Communications Server 2005 SP1. These previous products only provided IM without voice, so this architecture has been included inside the IM MCU through Office Communications Server 2007 and today's R2 version release.

### Web Conferencing MCU

Building on the success of Microsoft Office Live Meeting, one of the most popular online hosted Web conferencing solutions in the marketplace, OCS offers a Web Conferencing MCU that enables organizations with a hosted server-based internal Live Meeting conference server that runs within OCS. This allows organizations to host Live Meeting conferences on their internal infrastructure, which can be accessed by internal and remote users as well as external contacts. This Web Conferencing MCU gives the organization the ability to control meeting services within their own enterprise and to enable global meeting services that include audio, video, sharing of presentations and other data, as well as provide the ability to securely conference, communicate, and record these entire sessions for future research, retention, or compliance policies. The Microsoft Office Live Meeting service is also available in its existing Microsoft online-hosted format that companies or individuals can use to subscribe to as well. Offering both hosted and on-premise solutions for using Live Meeting is a clear differentiating factor between Microsoft and its competitors, such as GoToMeeting or AT&T Conferencing services, and sets the bar for the future of conferencing services. The only close competitor in this space would be WebEx with its EMX on-premise conferencing solution, which Cisco is currently using as its Web conferencing platform. But this is still a somewhat disconnected application, which does not allow users to integrate the conferencing service with other desktop tools.

What's also great about Live Meeting is the ability to escalate communications from a Microsoft Office or Information Worker perspective. For example, users can start with e-mail, progress to Instant Messaging for faster results, move on to multiparty voice and videoconferencing for even faster results, and ultimately engage in a Live Meeting session to really share a business idea or collaborate more effectively by sharing video, voice, and data. This progression is seamless through Microsoft's Unified Communications platform; these products integrate and work perfectly together.

### Office Communications Server Enterprise Edition

OCS Enterprise Edition is the full enchilada of voice, video, and conferencing. The most scalable version of OCS Enterprise Edition enables organizations to fully deploy a global Unified Communications solution by architecting a distributed network of OCS servers and performing backup and entire site failover functionality. By offering this open architecture, organizations can specify which servers are used for what functionality in regards to hosting audio/video, Instant Messaging, or Web conferencing on separate servers or on all three MCU components hosted on one server. Each Enterprise Edition server can be, and is architected to be, enabled for high-redundancy and failover in the format of clustering and network load balancing. Each OCS Enterprise Edition server can support thousands of users per server, but it is important to plan effectively for the number of users per MCU within a given environment.

To properly plan for an enterprise deployment, Microsoft released a planning wizard that can be used to determine the number of servers and provides additional planning information that you can download for free via http://www.microsoft.com/downloads. Simply search for "Planning Tool for Office Communications Server 2007."

The architecting of OCS server placement and which MCUs will be hosted on each OCS environment really depends on the number of users, locations, and requirements for backup and site failover per customer. Most Microsoft Unified Communications services partners, including my firm, provide **Architecture Design Sessions (ADS)**, which are typically one- to two-day sessions in which the services team meets with a customer alongside a Microsoft representative to architect a Unified Communications environment to fit the customer's needs. Using the Enterprise Edition of Microsoft OCS, you can scale out a global architecture to provide specific servers that host audio/video, Instant Messaging, and Web conferencing (see Figure 4.3). By scaling out this architecture, you can provide a geographically dispersed Unified Communications platform, connecting people, processes, and applications worldwide.

In this example, each server hosts an individual MCU to provide better bandwidth to users as well as to support the number of users required in each region. The Enterprise Edition of OCS uses a "pool" architecture to provide this level of scalability to enterprise organizations that demand it. Enabling a pool of OCSs allows organizations to not have to worry about failover or redundancy issues, which is the main difference between the Enterprise and Standard Editions of this software.

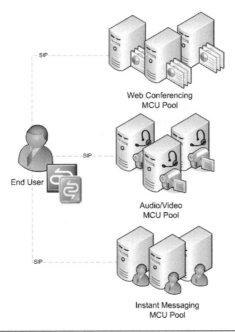

**FIGURE 4.3** Example of how Microsoft OCS can be architected using OCS Enterprise Edition

### Office Communications Server Standard Edition

In contrast to the OCS Enterprise Edition server architecture, OCS Standard Edition is a stand-alone server. OCS Standard Edition provides all the Instant Messaging, audio/video, and Web conferencing features out-of-the-box in one server, offering customers who do not have failover requirements a lightweight server to support a fair number of users per server. Obviously, you still need additional servers to support voice such as the OCS Mediation Server, but smaller departments or organizations can definitely utilize this simplified deployment solution to leverage the power of OCS in one physical machine. For detailed information on how many users are supported per server, the OCS planning tool, referenced earlier in this section, is exactly what you need.

What's great about the Standard Edition of OCS is that smaller companies or departments/divisions of larger enterprises that may not have the large number of users that would demand an OCS Enterprise Edition server can implement all-in-one Standard Edition servers internally to host the features that they require. OCS Standard Edition is also a great solution for companies during a Proof of Concept (POC) environment giving the company the ability to test and play with the features provided by OCS with a less lengthy deployment cycle in a sandbox or test environment, requiring little equipment and configuration.

To help you better understand OCS Standard Edition's role in an OCS environment, Figure 4.4 adds an OCS Standard Edition server in a couple of additional locations to enhance the OCS Enterprise Edition architecture illustrated previously in Figure 4.3.

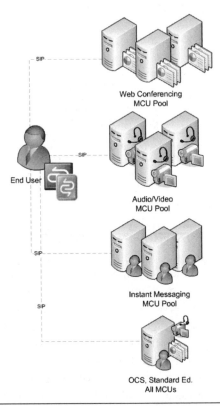

**FIGURE 4.4** OCS Standard Edition server added

In this example, OCS Standard Edition is used to host users in two new locations within the previously architected enterprise environment. What's great about the OCS design is that we can accommodate single office, multioffice, and multisite locations. Given that OCS as well as the entire Microsoft Unified Communications platform relies on Microsoft Active Directory, we can connect these networks together to provide shared directories in each location.

### Office Communications Server Edge Servers

Taking OCS to the next level, Microsoft provides three externally-facing Edge Servers to provide audio/video, Web conferencing, and SIP traffic over the Internet. Each of the three Edge Server roles are used within an OCS environment to provide federation with other OCS environments and federation with public IM networks including AOL, Yahoo, and Windows Live/MSN as well as to provide a server contact point for users who want to connect to an OCS server from outside the corporate network, but still want to be able to use voice, video, conferencing, and Instant Messaging. I like to call this server a "UC Freedom Server" in that it enables the full functionality of OCS both globally and remotely. Because I always work in a mobile environment, the OCS Edge Server roles are critical to me personally and to my organization as a whole. Together we can join conferences and invite outside contacts/partners to share voice, video, Instant Messaging, conferences, and data remotely, and we are still using a secure connection.

To build on the previously designed architecture, Figure 4.5 now adds an OCS Access Edge Server to connect remote users and enable the ability to federate between partner organizations and with the public IM networks such as AOL, Yahoo, and Windows Live/MSN as well as perform external voice access.

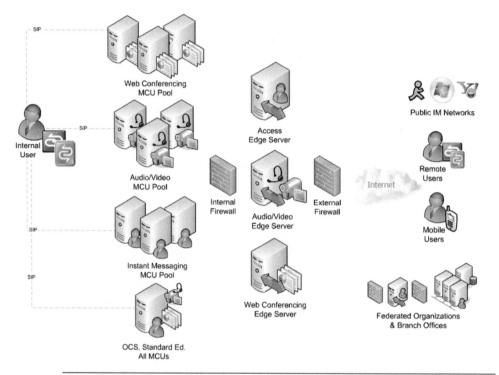

**FIGURE 4.5** OCS Access Edge Server added

It is also important to note the OCS Edge Server's equipment requirements. Whereas a normal OCS server, Enterprise or Standard Edition, requires a typical server hardware configuration, the OCS Edge Server requires more processing power, less data, and a dual Network Interface Card (NIC) card. The Edge Server does not store much data at all outside the configuration details of the server and the security certificates used to broker secure communications with partners and remote workers, so the type of server needed must factor in the number of connections required from the outside. A single OCS Edge Server for most enterprise organizations would not suffice because if thousands of users need remote access, they federate with multiple organizations, and they enable all their users to communicate with the public network, it would stretch this one server beyond its capability, although a single OCS Edge Server can handle 15,000 concurrent users for IM alone. What's great about the OCS Edge Server design is that you can architect and deploy an array of OCS Edge Servers to provide better bandwidth support as shown in Figure 4.6.

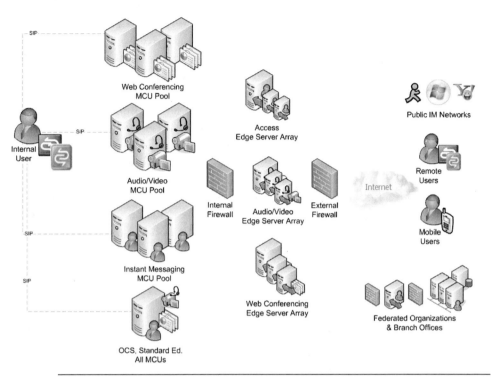

**FIGURE 4.6** Array of OCS Edge Servers

Another element critical to the OCS Edge Server as well as the entire OCS environment is how to configure the required Transport Layer Security (TLS) certificates on the server. As explained in Chapter 1, "The Communications Renaissance," TLS is the encryption used to secure communications within a SIP environment. Microsoft uses TLS within OCS to secure client and server communications by using TLS certificates. Each OCS server is configured with a server certificate, and client PCs or Macs are configured with a machine-level trusted root certificate to enable the clients to connect to an OCS server, whatever the role may be. From an OCS Edge Server perspective, two types of certificates are needed, public and private. Normally, an organization deploys internal TLS certificates on all the servers and client machines internally and then uses a publicly trusted certificate from companies such as a VeriSign, Entrust, and GoDaddy on the outside edge of the Edge Server. Remember when I mentioned that an OCS Edge Server requires two physical network ports? Well, within the management console of the OCS Edge Server you configure the private edge and public edge of this server. On the private edge, you configure a private IP address that provides the Edge Server with connectivity to the next-hop OCS server, which may be an OCS Director server, OCS Standard Edition server, or load balancer.

As depicted in Figure 4.7, you also configure one of the TLS server certificates from the internal Certificate Authority that you used for all your other internal OCS servers to safely and securely connect the OCS Edge Server internally. On the flip side, you configure the outside network port as the outside edge of the OCS Edge Server. From this side, you assign a public IP address that connects the OCS Edge Server to the public Internet and configure a public TLS certificate that can be trusted by remote users, federated partners, and the public IM networks including AOL, Yahoo, and Windows Live/MSN.

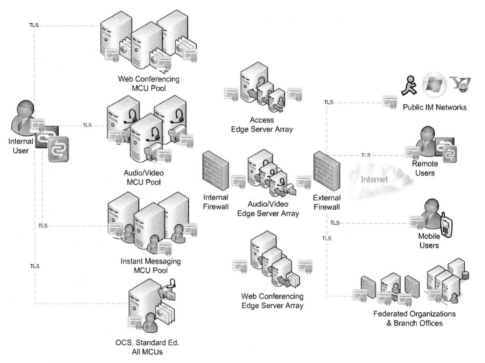

**FIGURE 4.7** Secured voice communications through TLS and MTLS

Did you imagine that such a single server configuration could do so much? Well, that's why Microsoft is a leader in the UC Magic Quadrant as reported by Gartner Research. Microsoft is able to consolidate and expose many features, out of the box, using software-powered VoIP, which leads us to our next OCS server role, the OCS Mediation Server, which is used for voice integration and SIP Trunking support for the OCS environment.

### Office Communications Server Mediation Server

The OCS Mediation Server is the most critical component in the current version of OCS, at this time, 2007 Release 2. The Mediation Server is used to connect the OCS environment to an external or internal telephony and VoIP environment. You would use the Mediation Server to connect to a media gateway device to connect a PBX to the OCS environment. This enables existing PBX users to use their existing extension and phone number from within the OCS client application, Office Communicator, as a Softphone or from an Office Communicator Phone Edition desk phone. This service also enables what is called dual-forking and simultaneous ring that enables all of your Office Communicator devices, mobile devices, and PBX phones to ring at the same time enabling you to decide how to answer the incoming call or defer the call to voicemail or another device.

The Mediation Server is also used to connect an OCS environment to a SIP Trunk. As mentioned earlier and explained in the section regarding Microsoft Response Point, a SIP Trunk is provided by an Internet Telephony Service Provider (ITSP). The ITSP SIP Trunk provides VoIP service to a Response Point Base Unit and now an OCS Mediation Server directly so that your clients can use Office Communicator applications via the PC, Mac, Web, or mobile to communicate using VoIP instead of using a PBX or POTS/analog lines.

Figure 4.8 depicts how the OCS Mediation Server is architected to connect to a PBX, SIP Trunk, and Gateway PSTN services.

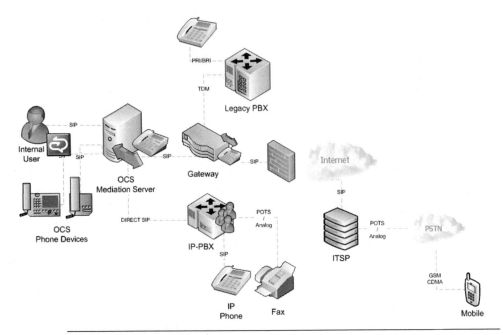

**Figure 4.8** OCS Mediation Server

The real Return on Investment (ROI) for implementing a Unified Communications environment, such as OCS, Exchange Server, and Live Meeting, has to do with the Mediation Server. PBX systems incur a tremendous payload in regards to recurring costs, upgrades, license fees, and as we are now seeing, extreme power consumption, which causes a dramatic expense in the data center to power and cool a PBX system and its required components as well as on the desk with a user's PBX phone. The same applies to the recurring monthly voice charges involved in using PSTN/POTS/analog and PBX-PSTN services. If you only use SIP Trunking and VoIP services, you pay a fraction of the cost on a monthly or annual subscription basis as well as still have the ability to communicate to the PSTN networks through the services provided by the ITSP. As mentioned earlier in the book, the ITSP provides VoIP-to-VoIP communication as well as connectivity to the PSTN network to communicate with mobile, landline, POTS or analog lines, as well as other companies that have PBX systems inhouse that have external VoIP or PSTN integration enabled. So you are not losing anything by implementing a fully VoIP integrated system in terms of functionality and reach, but are saving millions and ultimately billions of dollars in the enterprise. By implementing a voice solution using technology such as Microsoft's Unified Communications platform, you become the trusted advisor and the bottom line hero of your organization!

### Office Communications Server QoE Monitoring Server

As mentioned in Chapter 1, Quality of Experience (QoE) represents the overall quality of each user's experience within a voice communications environment. Microsoft uses QoE to ensure that not only the service itself is optimal, but that the users are happy as well. The Microsoft OCS QoE Monitoring Server is a free downloadable application that runs within the OCS environment and captures the experience of sessions that occur in real time and then reports the data of each session at the end of the session.

Figure 4.9 is an example of how the QoE Monitoring Server would be applied to a Unified Communications architecture.

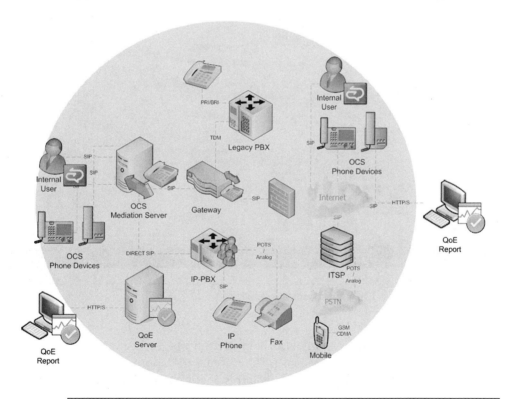

**FIGURE 4.9** QoE within a UC environment

As mentioned earlier in the book, most Telco providers are obsessed with the quality of the voice service itself and charge exorbitant fees for their high-quality QoS routers. Microsoft applies the same obsessiveness in respect to the quality of the service itself, but making sure that the end user is satisfied is the most important requirement in driving the overall success of a Unified Communications implementation.

Figure 4.10 is an example of a QoE report portal provided by the QoE Monitoring Server.

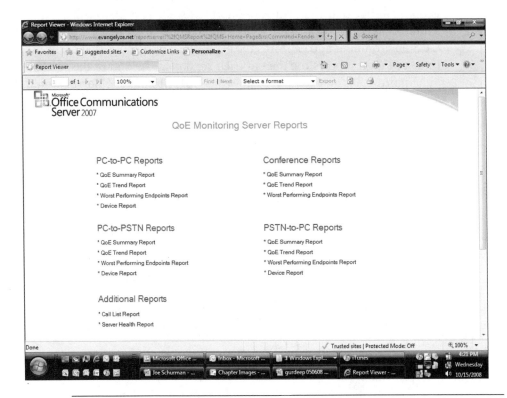

**FIGURE 4.10** OCS QoE Server Reports

These QoE reports also help identify the soft and hard ROI of the implemented voice system by identifying the appropriate level of quality for an organization to tweak its infrastructure to enable the proper level of optimal performance. Figure 4.11 is an example of a QoE report provided by the QoE Monitoring Server that aids in this process and analysis.

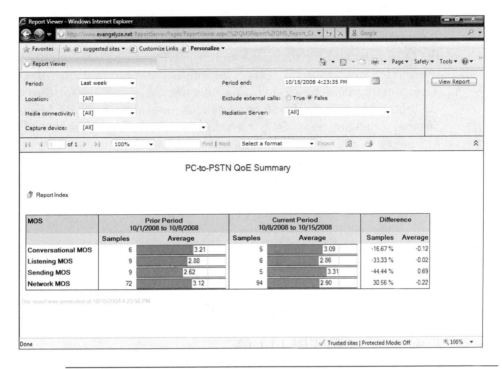

**FIGURE 4.11** Sample QoE report

## Office Communications Server Archiving Server

The OCS Archiving Server role provides the ability to record and archive conferencing and Instant Messaging sessions that take place within an OCS environment. There are three types of data you can archive within an OCS environment, including

- Call Detail Records (CDR)
- Instant Messages
- Live Meeting Conferencing Content

CDRs capture the history of voice calls that are made. These reports show the type of call made (PSTN, VoIP/SIP, internal) and show detail such as caller ID, account information for each user, duration of the call, and so on. The OCS Instant Messaging Archiving Service uses another

Windows-based technology called **Microsoft Message Queuing (MSMQ)**, which is a message delivery service that sends messages from the OCS front end servers to the archive server, which stores all the data transmitted during an IM session for internal and external IM sessions. Live Meeting conference archiving provides the capability to store the content, such as PowerPoint presentations, used during a Live Meeting session. Enabling these OCS recording and archiving services enables businesses to archive all their communications for the purposes of general retrieval and indexing for future research as well as for more tactical matters, such as compliance policies including, but not limited to, HIPPA, Sarbanes-Oxley, or other federal/governmental regulations.

Figure 4.12 depicts the OCS Archiving and CDR Server role configuration.

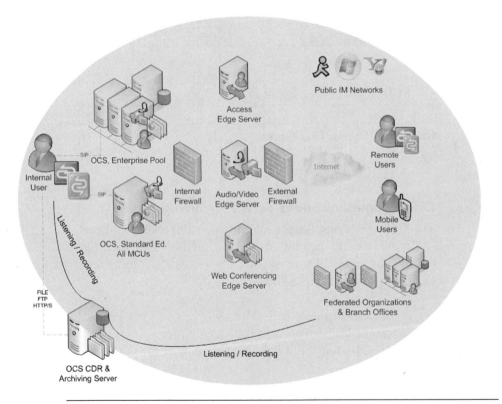

**FIGURE 4.12** OCS CDR & Archiving Server

Another flexible feature of the optional archiving and recording services provided within OCS is the reporting capability. All the data collected and stored is deposited into what is becoming the most popular and most used database server in the industry—Microsoft SQL Server. Using Microsoft SQL Server as the database store for all this information enables developers to create customized reports to show how the Unified Communications environment is being used, what kind of communications are being transmitted, and the details of those communications. This data can also be used to provide estimates of usage of services that can be identified as costs that can be tracked to show the executives and business owners the true ROI of the UC environment. More detail about how Microsoft SQL Server is used as the OCS back-end server role is explained in the next section.

### Office Communications Server Back-End Servers

As mentioned earlier, OCS uses Microsoft SQL Server as its back-end server role. The data stored in an OCS back-end server includes presence information, server configuration data, contact lists, block and allow settings, as well as archived information such as Instant Messaging sessions, Live Meeting conference recordings, and CDRs. The current version, OCS 2007 R2, requires that the OCS back-end server runs Microsoft SQL Server 2005 or 2008. If SQL Server is running on the same server as the OCS server, the platform support version must be 64-bit. Leveraging SQL Server database functionality enables high-performance features such as clustering and failover to provide a fast and scalable data network. Using SQL Server, you can also connect the data store to a Storage Area Network (SAN) system for even further storage capacity and record retention, which is common in most enterprises organizations.

To provide an example architecture of how Microsoft SQL Server would play a role in our fictitious Unified Communications environment, Figure 4.13 depicts the OCS back-end server role.

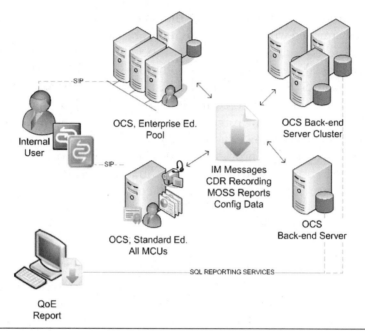

**FIGURE 4.13** OCS back-end data services

This architecture approach uses SQL server to provide data storage for the OCS servers as well as the OCS Archiving Service. The provided architecture also meets this enterprise organization's requirements for site failover and scalability.

### Office Communications Server Management Tools

Now you might ask, with all these different server roles that OCS enables, how would an organization manage all these different server configurations and settings? Great question. The answer is that you can't. Microsoft decided it would be best for you to figure this out on your own or hire resources to man each individual server for updates and configuration changes. Just kidding! There are actually two practical ways to manage an entire OCS environment using the following tools:

- Microsoft OCS Management Console
- Microsoft Systems Center

Without purchasing another Microsoft server product, the OCS Management Console that can run on a PC or can be opened from one of the OCS servers itself provides a management view of the entire OCS server environment and all its settings, minus the configuration settings of the OCS Edge Server. Because the OCS Access Edge Server does not live inside the internal network but is placed in a **Demilitarized Zone (DMZ)**, which is a network zone between the actual public Internet network and a company's internal network, a management console can be viewed from the servers individually using the Microsoft Windows Server management console (MMC).

Figure 4.14 is a screen shot of the OCS Management Console.

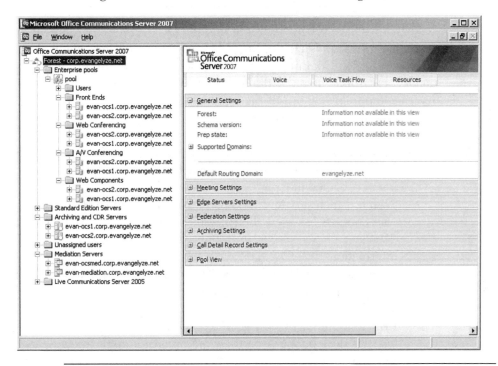

**FIGURE 4.14** OCS Management Console

If you want a collective snapshot of the OCS environment, minus the OCS Access Edge Server, along with your other enterprise servers within the company network, including SQL Servers, Exchange Servers, and so on, you can use Microsoft Systems Center. This product is not part of the Unified Communications platform but is a great management tool to use within a Microsoft network.

Both solutions work well and provide the capability to edit and update configuration settings for your OCS servers, but Microsoft Systems Center is a great tool to use to manage and monitor your entire Microsoft Unified Communications platform.

In September 2008, Microsoft released a free management pack called the Microsoft Office Communications Server 2007 Management Pack for Operations Manager 2007, which can be downloaded, for free, via the Microsoft Downloads Web site at http://www.microsoft.com/downloads.

# Microsoft Office Communicator

Now that we have provided insight into the OCS server environment, let's now take a look at what the end users of the system are enabled with! Microsoft Office Communicator is the client software used to connect to an OCS environment and is the feature-rich interface that enables users to leverage the following out-of-the-box highlighted features:

- Instant Messaging
- Presence of contacts to show their availability as well as enhanced presence showing a contact's status of being on the phone, in a conference, or in a meeting
- Search, which provides the ability to search contacts that are not in your contacts list, view their Presence availability, as well as contact details such as phone numbers, e-mail addresses, and other information
- Access to public IM networks (AOL, Yahoo, Windows Live/MSN)
- Peer-to-Peer audio and video sessions
- Voice calling features
- PBX Remote Call Control, which gives a user the ability to control his PBX desk phone from the Communicator application
- Dual-forking incoming calls to phones, PCs, and Communicator devices
- Conferencing access to Live Meeting
- Customized Presence (You customize your availability.)
- Recording of voice communications
- File transfer, which enables users to send files from one user to another internally and across firewalls
- Desktop sharing
- Multicontact audio and video conversations

n  Exchange distribution groups, which allow you to add company defined groups within Microsoft Exchange Server and Microsoft Active Directory to your contacts list as well as create on-the-fly meetings and conversations with an entire group at once.

The features listed previously are just a minor subset of the features available to end users through the Microsoft Office Communicator client application. For a full list of features, please visit http://www.microsoft.com/communicationsserver/en/us/capabilities.aspx. Office Communicator is available in four versions to extend functionality of the client application to the Web, phone, mobile device, PC, and even competitive Windows platforms such as the Mac OS X and BlackBerry devices.

## Office Communicator (PC Edition)

The default PC client version of Office Communicator enables full voice, video, and data access from one console to provide end users all the communication features they need to Instant Message; view Presence of contacts; communicate with internal and external contacts; share video, audio, and data; as well as have access to conferencing and voicemail from one application (see Figure 4.15).

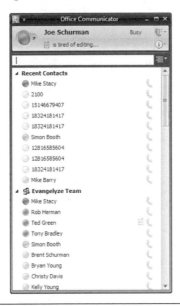

**FIGURE 4.15** Office Communicator client running on a Windows Vista PC

Once you have Communicator locked and loaded, innovation is at your
finger tips with the ability to Instant Message, start a voice call or an
audio/video session, share your desktop, start a conference call, start a
meeting, and much more as depicted in Figure 4.16 through Figure 4.23.

**FIGURE 4.16**  Presence and Out of Office

**FIGURE 4.17**  Instant Messaging

**FIGURE 4.18** Audio/video session

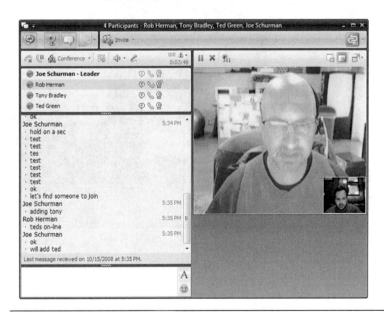

**FIGURE 4.19** Multiparty IM and audio/video session

**FIGURE 4.20** Voice call

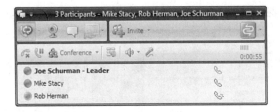

**FIGURE 4.21** Conference call

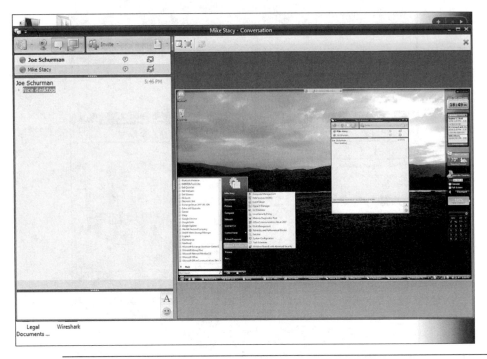

**FIGURE 4.22** Desktop sharing

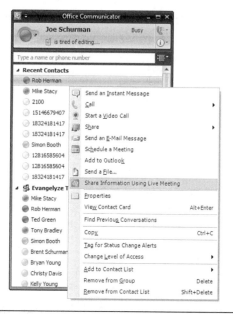

**FIGURE 4.23** Starting a meeting

## Office Communicator Attendant Console

The Communicator Attendant Console is the newest member to the Office Communicator client team, providing office secretaries or attendants with the ability to better manage incoming calls and conferences on behalf of their teams or executives through an intuitive software application that leverages Presence to show team and individual availability, enforcing the best means of contact for each.

Figure 4.24 shows a list of incoming calls and how an attendant would route these calls by dropping the incoming call to a specific person or team. The attendant can also apply notes based on speaking to the incoming caller and transferring the call along with the notes to the responsible party, providing additional intelligence to the communication.

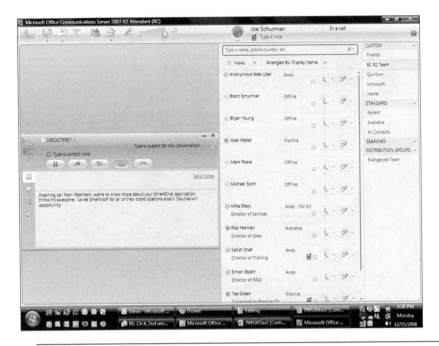

**FIGURE 4.24** Communicator Attendant Console

## Office Communicator Web Access

**Communicator Web Access (CWA)**, as shown in Figure 4.25, is a lightweight Communicator client version that enables Instant Messaging and Presence functionality via the Internet and, with the R2 release of Microsoft OCS, the ability to provide voice dial-back functionality as well as the extension of tabs for further application integration! Now, with the ability to join conference calls (have the conferencing server dial you back at your preferred number), this Web-based application merely highlights the focus of the Microsoft Voice and Unified Communications vision of software-powered voice and hosted services. This solution is really great for users who cannot install Communicator on their desktop or those who need to access Communicator from another computer or Web console. CWA supports Internet Explorer, Firefox, Safari, and Opera, which are the most widely used Web browsers in the industry, and this also provides Communicator with interoperability with an organization's users who may be running Unix, Linux, or other nonsupported desktop or server operating systems.

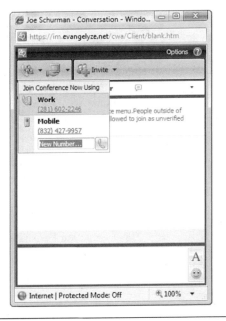

**FIGURE 4.25** CWA client

## Group Chat Client

The newly provided, and highly anticipated, Group Chat client now provides users with the ability to collaborate over topics that persist over time. Packed with chat rooms, archives, searching, and history discussions, the Group Chat client was a much awaited product from Microsoft within the unified communications platform. Through an acquisition of Parlano, a former Microsoft partner, Microsoft has further developed Parlano's previous group chat application and has made it a critical part of the Microsoft Unified Communications client product family.

As seen in Figure 4.26, the Group Chat application shows the ability to extend Presence through topic-based threads.

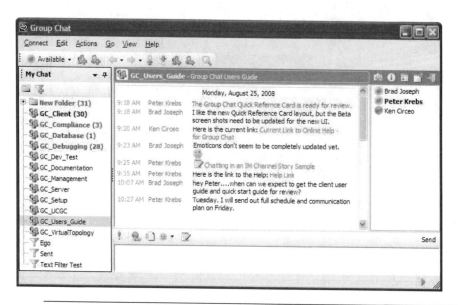

**FIGURE 4.26** Group Chat

## Office Communicator Mobile

**Communicator Mobile**, also known as **CoMo**, is an innovative mobile solution for Communicator that runs on both Microsoft Windows Mobile devices (as shown in Figure 4.27) as well as on competitive mobile devices such as the popular BlackBerry device, Nokia S40, and the Motorola RAZR, providing single-number reach to each device as well, making the cell phone an extension of the office phone. This client version of Office Communicator is similar to the CWA version in that it provides only Instant Messaging and Presence functionality on the device, but is great if you are a road warrior or simply want to be able to reach someone fast when you are on the run. One of the coolest features I have found in this version of Communicator is the ability to use the search feature to find contacts that are not in my contacts list to retrieve phone numbers, e-mail addresses, and other contact details. When I travel from one Microsoft office to another in countries all over the world, I meet with thousands of Microsoft employees and partners. I like knowing that if I need to meet someone at the office I am speaking at that day, I can easily find a local contact to either let me in the door or help me easily find resources at those specific facilities.

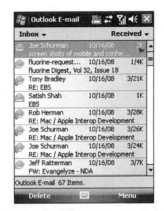

**FIGURE 4.27** Office Communicator Mobile application running on a Windows Mobile device

## Office Communicator Phone Edition

The Communicator Mobile client and the Communicator Phone Edition client are often mistaken for one another. Whereas the Communicator Mobile application version is specific to mobile devices, Microsoft partnered with several OEM vendors that have designed Communicator-specific phone devices that run a version of Communicator on the specific device. The first OEM device to market was the LG|Nortel IP8540 phone device, an actual phone that runs the Communicator client on the phone and has a bright screen that displays all your Communicator contacts with their Presence availability directly via the screen, which is also touch-enabled to allow users to call contacts directly via a push of the finger (see Figure 4.28).

**FIGURE 4.28** Microsoft Office Communicator Phone Edition running on an
LG | Nortel IP8540 device

## Microsoft Messenger for Mac OS X

I have to be honest. The Mac Messenger 7.1 client, which enables
Communicator functionality for the Mac OS X, is the coolest
Communicator client out of the stack—even though it does not enable
Remote Call Control for PBX integration or VoIP calling capability outside
the OCS environment. This client alone allows me to integrate Presence
within my Mac Book Air running the latest version of the Mac Office suite,
with Mac Office 2008. The client is nicely developed as with all Mac OS X
applications and really answers the question of Microsoft's ability to inter-
operate with competitive platforms and applications. Integrated with Mac
Entourage 2008, I can see the status availability of my corporate and personal contacts as well as participate in audio, video, and data sharing sessions internally and outside the corporate network. Many people say that
Microsoft technology runs better on a Mac, and that is definitely the case
in my experience. On top of these cool features, the client is absolutely free
and downloadable via the Microsoft downloads Web site http://www.
microsoft.com/downloads. Search for "Mac Messenger 7.1" and try it out
for yourself.

Figure 4.29 through Figure 32 show the user interface for the
Microsoft Messenger client for the Mac.

**FIGURE 4.29** Microsoft Messenger for Mac OS X

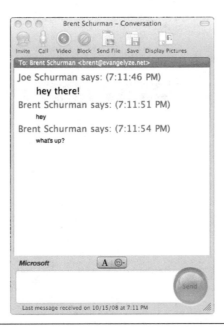

**FIGURE 4.30** Instant Messaging session

**FIGURE 4.31** Audio/video session

**FIGURE 4.32** Incoming call notification

Providing multiple versions of the Communicator client enables greater reach across different operating systems, Web applications, and devices to provide anywhere access to voice, video, and data, and truly provide a Unified Communications solution.

## Microsoft Office Live Meeting

As mentioned earlier in the overview of the OCS Conferencing MCU, Microsoft Office Live Meeting is Microsoft's most innovative conferencing solution to date and slaughters the competition including Web-Ex, which has been the most popular Web conferencing application in the industry.

Adding to this innovative brilliance, Microsoft released a Microsoft hardware device in its release of the Microsoft Office RoundTable conferencing device. This device connects to a PC via a USB connection and serves as a video and voice device for the Live Meeting conference through either the hosted on-premise Conferencing MCU through OCS or through the Microsoft hosted-online Live Meeting Service. The device has a series of cameras and mirrors on the top part of the device that captures a video of each meeting participant around the device and then displays these participants in a panoramic view of the Live Meeting client application. If you need to join a team meeting remotely or if you are setting up RoundTable meetings from one site to another, you can see a panoramic view of everyone in the conference room as well as see the active speaker in the provided active speaker window with the shared data and presentations in the middle of the screen (see Figure 4.33).

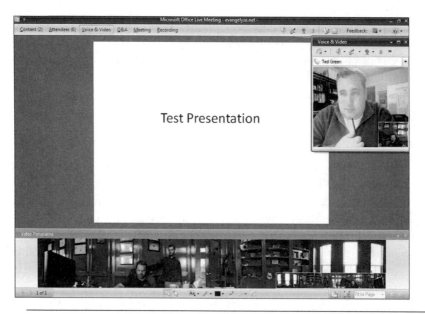

**FIGURE 4.33** Live Meeting client showing participants and speaker

Live Meeting also enables cross-firewall connectivity so that you are able to host RoundTable sessions between partners, customers, and internal remote sites without any Web configuration needed. Talk about innovative, this is the future of real-time communication and lessens the burden of cost and time away from the office when you must travel. With energy costs rising and technology such as this available, there will not be as much of a need to attend meetings in person because you can see, communicate, and share documents and presentations as if you were sitting in a conference room or office location on-site.

## Microsoft Exchange Server

Although not really a VoIP product, Microsoft Exchange Server is at the forefront of the Unified Communications platform in providing features such as enterprise mail, calendar, and contacts, but more importantly as it affects Unified Communications overall—Unified Messaging and Voice access to the Exchange Server. To be honest, my team on the Real Time

Collaboration (RTC) incubation team would have taken a different course within the large business group silos at Microsoft had it not been for the Exchange Server team's willingness to include us in their run for Unified Communications. Most of the marketing budget, development, integration, and sales revenue generation are funneled directly through the industry's most respected and market dominating e-mail server platform.

The following are features of Microsoft Exchange Server with its 2007 Service Pack 1 release:

- Enterprise E-mail
- Enterprise Calendar
- Enterprise Contacts
- Unified Messaging (voicemail/e-mail integration)
- Presence
- Click-to-Call
- Integration with Microsoft Office Live Meeting
- Integration with Microsoft Office Communicator
- 64-bit operating system support
- Windows Server 2008 and Hyper-V support

## Unified Messaging

With the release of Microsoft Exchange Server 2007, Service Pack 1 (SP1), Exchange Server enables the capability to receive voice messages within your e-mail inbox similar to how we explained the features of Unified Messaging within Microsoft Response Point. Exchange Server provides more advanced Unified Messaging services than Response Point in that the server provides synchronization with the e-mail client to review played messages, communicating back to the voicemail system that the message has been reviewed. In Microsoft Response Point, you have to delete the message or review the message on your phone itself to update the system that the voicemail has been reviewed.

By configuring the Unified Messaging server role within Microsoft Exchange Server 2007, SP1, Exchange Server becomes the organization's voicemail server as well as an organization's enterprise e-mail and calendar server. Figure 4.34 depicts how a voice call and voicemail message are generated through a Microsoft Exchange Server Unified Messaging environment.

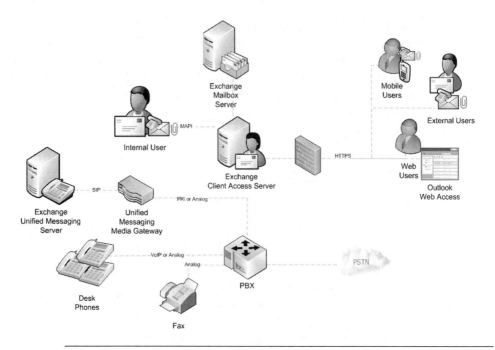

**FIGURE 4.34** Microsoft Exchange Voice Architecture

Exchange Server provides a powerful voicemail platform in that if a voice message is left in your Exchange voicemail account, a message is generated from the Exchange Server to your client application via e-mail, whether you are using a mobile device, PC, or Web browser (see Figure 4.35). If you don't have access to a PC, you can call into your Exchange Server from your phone and have the server read out your messages and calendar events.

You can also check your voicemail and calendar via a Windows Mobile device, the ever-popular iPhone, and from a Web browser. Exchange Server's Outlook Web Access solution for the 2007 SP1 version allows you to review your voicemail from within Firefox, Safari, Internet Explorer, and even Opera and other supported browsers through Outlook Web Access, as shown in Figure 4.36.

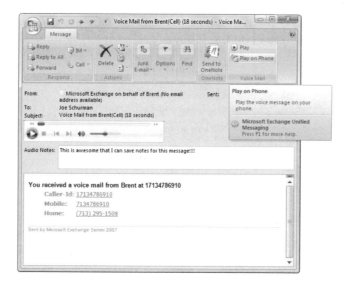

**FIGURE 4.35** Microsoft Office Outlook 2007 voice and message

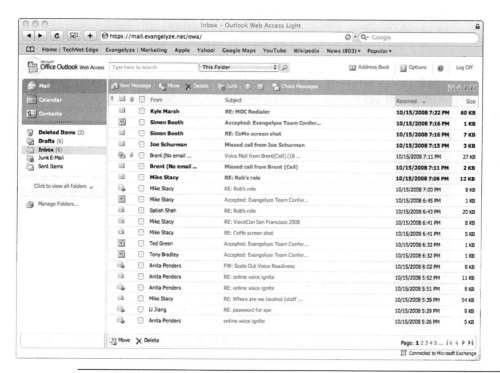

**FIGURE 4.36** Outlook Web Access

Extending the reach even further, you can pick up the same voicemail message via e-mail on the iPhone, as shown in Figure 4.37.

**FIGURE 4.37** Retrieve voicemail via e-mail on an iPhone

## Microsoft Office Live Meeting and Communicator Integration

With the Microsoft Office Live Meeting 2007 add-in toolbar, scheduling Web conferences from within Outlook 2007 is a breeze. Using the toolbar, you can create a Live Meeting hosted conference using the public Live Meeting service online, a hosted Live Meeting conference via the OCS, or a conference call using your conference bridge or using a Communicator call enabling a ton of flexibility for a business user (see Figure 4.38).

This capability of a one-click conference solution is a Web-Ex and competitive online Web conferencing killer. With this add-in toolbar to Live Meetings, a business user is enabled with a flexible conferencing solution with one-click access.

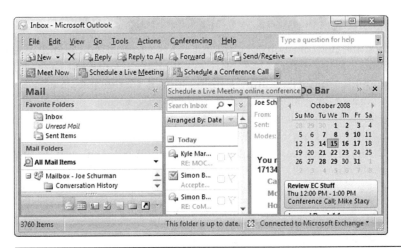

**FIGURE 4.38** Microsoft Office Live Meeting toolbar within Microsoft Office Outlook

With the Office Communications Server 2007 R2 release, users now have the ability to leverage dial-in conferencing to host their own conference calls via the OCS conferencing server functionality, cutting costs dramatically. Through my organization, we obtained a Direct Inward Dialing (DID) number from our ITSP provider which we leveraged for outside callers to reach our OCS conferencing server remotely and applied the setting through the new menu provided within the Live Meeting setup console, as seen Figure 4.39.

**FIGURE 4.39** Dial-in conferencing settings within Live Meeting (hosted)

## Calling Features within Outlook 2007

If someone told you a couple of years ago that you could use telephone functionality within Outlook, you would have looked at them funny. Oddly enough, there is a feature within Outlook that enables a user to dial out to a contact or connect to voicemail directly within the Outlook client that leverages the voice features of Communicator and OCS. Figure 4.40 is an example of how you can Click-to-Call a contact directly from within your Outlook inbox based on the recognition of a phone number by the client application itself.

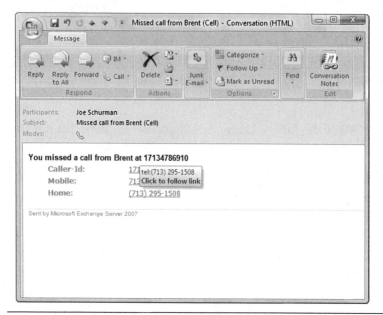

**FIGURE 4.40** Microsoft Office Outlook Missed Call Notification

## Microsoft Exchange Server Push E-mail for Outlook Mobile

One feature missing for years in the Exchange Server platform is the push e-mail feature provided by the BlackBerry Enterprise Server platform, giving BlackBerry devices the competitive edge over other e-mail devices in the industry. Push e-mail is nothing new to Microsoft as it has been in existence since the release of Microsoft Exchange Server 2003 SP2. This feature is a built-in service even today with Microsoft Exchange Server 2007 that provides instant e-mail transmittal to mobile devices and applications as soon as new mail is received. Goodbye, BlackBerry! No longer do enterprise organizations have to purchase additional server equipment and software licenses from RIM, the manufacturer of the BlackBerry devices and BlackBerry Enterprise Server, to enable instant e-mail delivery. A most notable recent release was the announcement of the Apple iPhone's support for Microsoft Exchange Server's push e-mail feature, giving the most innovative phone in history a corporate look and feel. I hope to see more of this innovation from a mobile perspective take place over the next few years, wiping RIM out of the market. For more detailed information about my views on this matter, feel free to read my *Pocket PC* magazine article of April 2006, titled, "BlackBerry vs. Windows Mobile, Battle for the Enterprise." It's about time these predictions came true!

Figure 4.41 depicts the user interface via Outlook Mobile for Windows Mobile devices.

**FIGURE 4.41** Microsoft Outlook Mobile for Windows Mobile

## Microsoft Unified Communications Devices

I talk a lot about the power of virtual PBX systems and Softphone devices, but I will say, some of the devices that Microsoft and Microsoft's partners have produced as of late are just flat out cool. As mentioned earlier, Microsoft produced a beautiful conferencing device with the RoundTable, but Microsoft's OEM partners such as Nortel, Polycom, NEC, Jabra, Samsung, ViTELiX, and even some of the devices on the horizon that have yet to be released are amazing. What's even cooler is that with the power of OCS, I can acquire any of these devices and sign into my account to leverage the VoIP features explained throughout this book. What's also cool (my son Davis loves this) is the ability to see all these devices ring at the same time when an incoming call comes through.

One of my favorite UC photos is the one of Gurdeep Singh Pall, whose commentary is included in this book, sitting at a desk full of these devices. I actually used the image shown in Figure 4.42 in an article I wrote for *Redmond* Magazine in the November 2007 issue.

**FIGURE 4.42** Gurdeep Singh Pall, Microsoft Corporate VP, UC Group, with UC devices

To download your own images of these devices, visit http://www.microsoft.com/presspass/presskits/uc/gallery.mspx.

## Microsoft Entourage 2008 for Mac OS X

Another brilliant move by Microsoft was providing Exchange Server access from a Mac OS X operating system. Through the Microsoft Mac Office 2008 platform, Microsoft Entourage provides the ability to connect to multiple Microsoft Exchange Servers, something that cannot be done within one Microsoft Office Outlook profile on the PC, and enables Presence, Unified Messaging access, as well as access to corporate contacts, distribution groups, and sharing of calendars (see Figure 4.43).

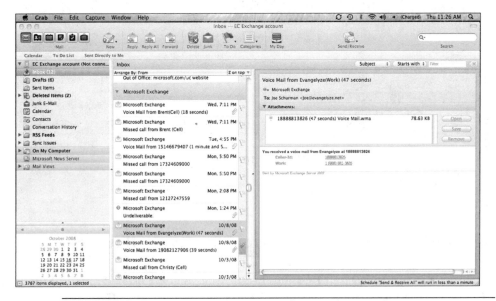

**FIGURE 4.43** Microsoft Entourage client running on Mac OS X

What's even cooler, and the main reason why I provided an interview for the TechNet Edge team, is the fact that through Microsoft Entourage 2008 for the Mac, I can add multiple Microsoft Exchange Server accounts, which is something not currently possible with Microsoft Office Outlook. Taking this a step further, the calendar on the Mac can pull in my schedule from multiple accounts, synchronizing them all into one view! That's just brilliant! In addition to the Microsoft Office 2008 suite for the Mac, the Entourage client also comes with a handy tool called My Day, as shown in Figure 4.44. This application shows a review of my daily schedule combining multiple Microsoft Exchange Server calendars and my personal calendar.

**FIGURE 4.44** My Day application on my MacBook Air

## Microsoft Exchange E-mail for the Apple iPhone

Let me repeat that I used to be an Apple hater. I used Windows Mobile, I was a heavy Zune user, and "I am proud to be a PC." However, I decided to give the Apple iPhone a trial run, still keeping my Verizon Wireless Motorola Q Windows Mobile 6.0 device. The end result was that I liked the iPhone so much, I canceled my Verizon service and purchased iPhones for my entire family two days later. I still use a PC—I run Office on a PC and a Mac—but to be truly honest, the iPhone just completely slaughters Microsoft's integrated portable music and mobility platform. I even bit the bullet and repurchased all the same music I had on my Zune account via my new iTunes account, which was a major pain, but it is worth having everything in the palm of my hand.

Figure 4.45 shows the E-mail Account settings menu on the iPhone.

**FIGURE 4.45** Exchange E-mail Account setup page via iPhone

More importantly Microsoft Exchange mobile e-mail on the iPhone is nice, clear, vibrant, and easy to read and respond to (see Figure 4.46). I also like the quick ability to respond, mark as unread, and other features that take a few more clicks on a Windows Mobile device. And a few more clicks for me is a no-go—that is my number one pet peeve. Additionally, the iPhone was the first to the market on mobile devices for threaded SMS text messaging, so when you don't want to use e-mail, you can easily text single or multiple contacts easily and review the thread later on.

**FIGURE 4.46** My sample Exchange push e-mail via the iPhone

# The Microsoft Unified Communications Vision

The information contained in this chapter only outlines the products that are available today as part of the Microsoft Unified Communications platform. To truly understand where the future of the UC vision is taking place, you have to look at what is happening from a software and services perspective. In the future, nobody cares where the dial tone is coming from and end users will have an enormous selection of desktop and handheld devices to choose from. What sets UC manufacturers competing in this space apart? Software+Services. Through S+S, Microsoft is providing application developers with the tools that will enable them to develop voice-enabled Line of Business applications that will transform the way businesses operate by integrating voice and unified communications solutions into their business processes. In addition to this, Web services and hosted Unified Communications solutions will be available for organizations to outsource their communications infrastructure to key hosting providers as well as leverage Web services to connect to networks and markets they could not connect to before. This is the future of Unified Communications. This is the Communications Renaissance.

As mentioned before, I have been involved with the Microsoft Unified Communications business, marketing, product development, field services, and sales teams for the past eight years. But a turning point came when I watched Steve Ballmer, Microsoft CEO, step on stage in front of thousands of attendees at the Microsoft Worldwide Partner Conference in Houston, Texas, and state that UC is one of Microsoft's top four investments for the 2009 fiscal year. It was then, that the several hundred thousands of dollars that I invested to start an enterprise voice practice, the writing of this book and my previous books, and the time spent developing products and relationships over the past eight years really felt worthwhile. In that one second where Ballmer, nearly screaming with enthusiasm, stated this focus, I finally felt confident in the strategy my team and I bet on years ago. It is now, with the support of the Microsoft Unified Communications Group, its key partners, and the Microsoft field, that we can show the world this new transformation of voice communications through the power of software.

# CHAPTER 5

# Simply Speaking: The Integration of Speech Recognition with Voice and Unified Communications

*Speech vision statement by XD Huang, General Manager, Microsoft Research Communications Innovation Center*

Early on, Microsoft's initial investment in speech recognition technology was to provide individuals with the ability to customize the interaction between a user and an operating system to perform tasks saving keystrokes and time. Over many years, much work was put into multilanguage support, ease of use in regards to end-user speech training to enhance the recognition process, and then the application of providing programming templates to enable developers to integrate speech into their applications.

Fortunately, there existed a man, professor, and mentor with a vision to take speech recognition even further by adding speech into not so obvious places such as telephone devices, telephony interactive voice response (IVR) systems, and other cool applications. This man, this professor, this mentor is Xuedong Huang. XD, as he is known, is now the General Manager of the prestigious Microsoft Research Communications Innovation Center in Redmond, Washington. His latest project, Microsoft Response Point, provides speech recognition in small business phone systems.

Within this chapter, we will explore the innovations within speech technology throughout Microsoft's Voice and Unified Communications products, highlighting the vision of XD Huang.

# The Vision of Speech within Microsoft's VoIP Products and Services

Before I met XD in November 2005, I did not know what to expect. I was nervous about meeting him as I had heard of XD through my experience working with the Unified Communications Group, known at that time as the Real-time Communications group or RTC team. The opportunity to work at Microsoft Research was one of the coolest things that had happened to me in my previous 13 years of working with Microsoft. At my first meetings with the Communications Innovation Center in Redmond, I was to provide feedback and become familiar with a new communications product that would serve as a small business IP Phone System, then called by its code name "Edinburgh," now known as Microsoft Response Point. The prototype I was privy to then was a black box that looked like a cable box for television and the ugliest phone I had ever seen. Surrounding this technology were experts from various areas of Microsoft including JJ Cadiz, Bob Taniguchi, Robert Brown, Li Jiang, Regi John, Jayman Dalhal, and XD Huang among others. When I met the team, I immediately knew that the next several years were going to be interesting. XD, one of the most remarkable technologists I have met, provided an overview of what the vision of the CIC and Edinburgh was, and it was up to me to build a readiness and training plan for partners to launch this product off the ground. To provide a better understanding of his vision of this product and others, XD gave me a vision document, titled "Voice Communications 3.0," which had been published internally and reviewed by Bill Gates himself as Bill has been heavily involved with the team since the beginning—even though I have never met Bill personally.

Given XD's extensive experience in the areas of speech and VoIP, I think it is important to capture XD's vision of the future of speech services and how they will provide further innovation in the future of voice and unified communications technologies. The following are XD's direct comments:

*"My vision on voice communications is that voice is the most natural way for people to communicate, which will enable us to bring a wide range of devices to the web 3.0 era. VOIP helps this cause and provides a means for us to bring people and devices together."*

*—XD Huang, General Manager, Communications Innovation Center, Microsoft Corporation*

# Microsoft Voice and Speech Integration

Building on XD's vision, Microsoft tightly and innovatively integrated speech recognition technology within many of its enterprise and small business products. The evolution of this integration began with a separately sold product for enterprise customers called Microsoft Speech Server. With Microsoft Speech Server, customers had the ability to develop, enable, and integrate speech integration within their line of business applications for the purposes of providing IVR for phone systems, accessibility solutions for the disabled, or to speed up the process of applications by using voice commands. This server, managed by XD's team, gave developers the opportunity to build on an open platform to integrate speech in ways previously not thought possible.

As of 2007, Microsoft discontinued Speech Server as a separate server product and decided to open the platform internally to allow Speech Server to be enabled in several Microsoft products. We now see the speech engine technology within our PCs and mobile devices, but from a communications perspective, Microsoft provided speech integration within two voice and unified communications products with Microsoft Office Communications Server 2007, now in its R2 release, and Microsoft Response Point, currently in version 1, Service Pack 2. The following is an overview of how speech configuration and development are enabled within these two Microsoft Voice and Unified Communications products.

## Microsoft Office Communications Server Speech Integration

With the announcement of "Live Server," the beta name of Office Communications Server 2007, came the death of Microsoft Speech Server as a separate Microsoft server product licensed and sold by Microsoft. Speech Server's new role is to make available its engine through a series of SDKs and APIs to other Microsoft products including both Microsoft Exchange Server and Microsoft Office Communications Server in the Microsoft Unified Communications platform and for developers to create custom speech recognition formulas and processes to handle requests via voice. In regards to how Office Communications Server (OCS) uses this technology, the speech server toolset enables developers to create custom IVR prompts and processes to handle call flow and automated call distribution (ACD).

5. SIMPLY SPEAKING

Figure 5.1 is an example of a sample IVR process that can be configured using Microsoft Office Visio to customize the way incoming calls are
handled for a company.

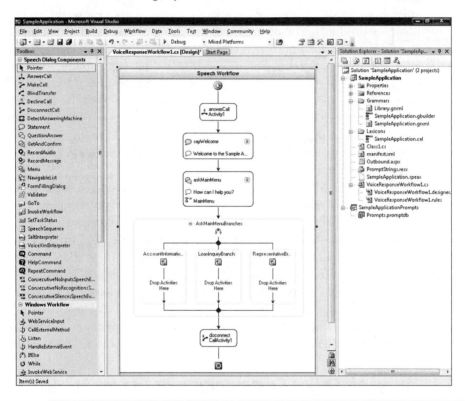

**FIGURE 5.1** Automated Call Distribution example (Microsoft Visio)

After the process is completed and saved, the template is then used by
OCS to process incoming calls. In this example, if an external caller needs
to reach the IT help desk, a call distribution process is enabled to move the
caller to this template in which the caller will reach another set of
voice/speech-enabled menus to reach the appropriate party within the
organization to handle this incoming request. Enabling this capability,
helps organizations provide better service to their customers and partners
as well as provides better efficiency in regards to ensuring that calls are
routed to the appropriate contact with the right skill set or job role to handle the request.

By far, the most powerful speech integrated service within the Microsoft Unified Communications platform is the user's ability to call into the Microsoft Exchange Server leveraging the Unified Messaging and Outlook Voice Access components. Through this feature, calendar, e-mail, contacts, and so on are made available to users via voice. Through speech recognition and voice prompts, the service can manipulate your calendar, e-mail, contacts, and so on as well. For example, my organization has deployed the Microsoft Exchange Server Unified Messaging solution, and we have the Outlook Voice Access service running as well. When I am mobile, I can call into my account and the Exchange Server can tell me what meetings and calls I have remaining for the day. If there is a reason to do so, and I have done this before, I can tell the service to clear my calendar for the day and the server will not only remove my meetings for that date, but also inform the participants of each meeting that I had to cancel. The same process works if I am running late to a meeting, and with the traffic in Houston, Texas, that happens a lot. In this situation, I can tell the service I'm running 15 minutes late and the service will adjust the meeting and/or simply inform the participants of the meeting that I'm running late. Hmm, what did we do here? We just eliminated the need for a personal assistant! Figure 5.2 depicts how this server-based architecture works.

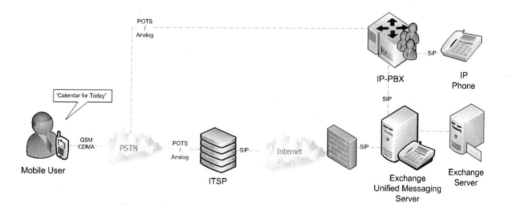

**FIGURE 5.2** Exchange Voice Access architecture

Microsoft Office Communications Server speech recognition also handles all supported language packs to enable enterprise voice and communications in any language. Also, no voice training is needed by users to educate the system on their voice and how they communicate, which saves time and provides a quick on-ramping process for customers to begin taking advantage of services such as voice-dialing, custom call routing plans, and so on.

## Microsoft Response Point and Speech Recognition

Taking speech to an entirely new level, the Microsoft Communications Innovation Center decided to take "speech to the street" in respect to enabling speech recognition within the phone devices themselves. Microsoft Response Point, as mentioned earlier in the book and in XD's vision document, is an innovative IP Phone System for small businesses and now branch offices. Each certified OEM Response Point phone device is enabled with a Response Point blue button that, when pressed, gives the person using the phone the ability to tell the phone what they want it to do—whether placing a call, transferring a call, and so on.

Microsoft Response Point also has a speech recognition-enabled automated attendant that allows external callers to reach groups, locations, and individuals via voice as well. This great feature comes at no additional cost to the customer and provides the customer a virtual built-in operator. Using Response Point Administrator, you also can customize the way these calls are answered and handled. You also can customize the welcome greeting and improve efficiency by offering answers to frequently asked questions that external callers might have, such as what are the company's hours, fax number, and location.

Configuring ACD and the Automated Attendant service within Microsoft Response Point is easy. Figure 5.3 is a screen shot of the Microsoft Response Point Administrator management console that allows you to customize these settings.

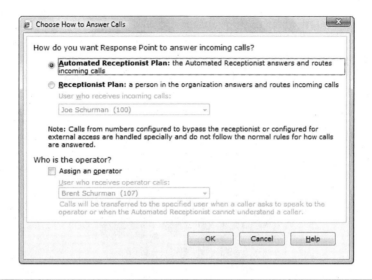

**FIGURE 5.3** Microsoft Response Point Administrator call distribution settings

Figure 5.4 is an example of how to use Microsoft Response Point Administrator to customize answers to frequently asked questions from external callers.

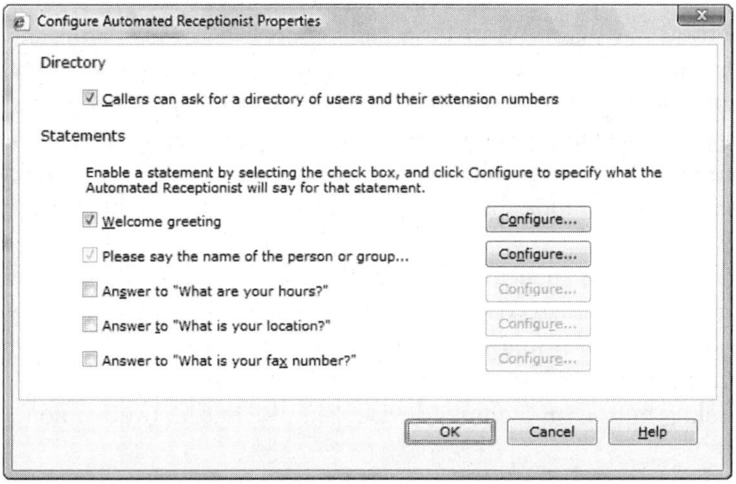

**FIGURE 5.4** Microsoft Response Point Automated Receptionist Properties

As mentioned earlier, for end users, each Microsoft Response Point phone is enabled with a blue Response Point button, also known as the "Magic Blue Button," as shown in Figure 5.5. There is even a Web site called themagicbluebutton.com as well! This button, when pressed, dials the Response Point Base Unit device and then enables the user or caller to say the name or extension of the person he is trying to reach.

**Figure 5.5** Microsoft Response Point Magic Blue Button (on each OEM phone device)

The Response Point button can also be used during a call to park a call, retrieve a call, and transfer a call. For a list of voice commands, the user can say "What can I say," and the system responds with available voice commands. The system does not need to be trained, can be used to voice-dial contacts in your Microsoft Office Outlook or Windows contact list by importing contacts, and ensures that you never drop a transferred call, never have to look for a number again, and overall simplifies your phone experience.

Providing such a user friendly interface to enable administrators to quickly customize voice-enabled commands for an IP Phone system is just one of the latest innovations to come out of Redmond and puts Microsoft ahead of the competition in providing an innovative feature as a voice-dialing button on a phone device. Simple, but innovative nonetheless!

# The Future of Speech with Voice-Enabled Applications

We are already seeing how speech recognition is changing the way people communicate. This is all made possible by software and solid speech recognition engines that make voice training the process of the past and the configuration of how voice commands are handled seamlessly.

In the future, based on my work with Microsoft Research and providing competitive analysis and research through my firm, the next big wave of speech recognition in voice communications products will primarily be fourfold:

- **Translation**. I think the next big wave of speech recognition will be intelligent translation services. In the near future, I hope to see the ability to communicate with a voice and unified communications endpoint such as a Microsoft Office Communications Server Phone Edition or Mobile Edition device and have the device translate my speech to the other calling party or conference participants in the language they prefer. I also see the functionality of intelligently translating speech to text for Instant Messaging, SMS, and e-mail as well.

- **Intelligent automation**. In the near future, I expect to see voice automation such as the ability to speak a command and have the computer or device I am speaking into intelligently route or automate my requests. For example, in the movie *Iron Man* Tony Stark's automated assistant, JARVIS, is a speech-enabled, voice recognition system that responds to native language and can process tasks easily by understanding subtasks dependent on the initial request. If Tony says something, the system responds and knows how to provide feedback based on understanding Tony's intent. If Tony is in a conversation and then ends the conversation with an actual task or command, JARVIS knows what to do. Currently, we have to be extremely specific and spend a lot of time training a speech system to understand our intent, pretty much negating the time we were looking to save using the system.

- **Consumer-focused solutions**. To date, Microsoft has made significant investments in voice communications technology for small businesses and enterprise organizations. In the near future, I believe that new, innovative, and affordable voice communications solutions and devices will be made available to consumers either tied into the Windows Live platform or another source platform. I would like to see home automation technology integrated into this as well so that my home communications is tied into my entire media, security, lighting, air conditioning, and other controls within my home based on speech integration, time-based controls, and remote management.

As an example of the use of speech APIs and SDKs made available now through the Microsoft Developer Network, our organization is taking speech to a different level and helping those in need of speech-to-text and text-to-speech capability through one of our Evangelyze Communications SmartSuite applications. This application was designed to help hearing-impaired individuals to participate in voice conference calls. Through software-powered voice within Microsoft Office Communications Server, we have created the ability, through the Microsoft Office Communicator application (an extension), for users to join a conference call. Their voices are represented via text that they enter into the Communicator application. Through this interface, callers who are not hearing-impaired are able to hear what the user entered as text into the Communicator application as voice on the conference call in any language. All conversations that are provided by callers on the conference call are then returned back to the Communicator client application in a separate extension of the application that shows the text translated from speech back to the hearing-impaired user. Through this scenario, we are able to leverage speech recognition and translation technology simply through software to enable the unthinkable. Taking this a step further, we are developing the same capability for any individual to participate in a conference call that may require a language that the caller cannot speak natively. The caller can then use Communicator to join the conference call and participate by entering their conversation via text in the language they prefer into Communicator, and then the text is translated via voice in the language in which the other callers are speaking. The same translation is provided back to the caller in the language of his or her preference from the other callers on the conference line. Now, that is freaking cool!

Using these simple examples, you can see what is possible in the areas of speech with voice and unified communications products. We are only seeing early stages of this development today, and I anticipate that major speech technology breakthroughs will occur within the next two years that will make a drastic impact on voice and unified communications applications and devices in this industry. I am confident that Microsoft will execute some of these extremely innovative new services and products within the next fiscal year, and I know that consumers and businesses alike will be amazed about what is to come in regards to providing simple, slick, affordable, and highly innovative voice communications!

# CHAPTER 6

# VOICE COLLABORATION

In 2005, I wrote a book titled *Professional Live Communications Server 2005* published by Wrox Books. One of my favorite chapters in that book and one of my favorite topics when discussing Microsoft's collaboration products and services is how these products and services integrate with our daily activities. Most businesses run the ever-popular and most dominant information worker suite on the planet—Microsoft Office. Now, in its 2007 release, Microsoft Office offers business workers, students, and even home users the most innovative collaborative platform in the marketplace, connecting applications, devices, and more importantly people on a global scale.

With the power of voice and unified communications integration with the Microsoft Office suite, the possibilities are endless. This chapter focuses on how Microsoft Office connected to voice and unified communications products and services provides organizations and individuals a solution that has absolutely no competition.

## Microsoft Office and Voice

As explained previously, the key differentiating factor between Microsoft and other voice and unified communications competitors lies within the integration of applications that users leverage on a daily basis. Combining Microsoft Office's required functionality—Word documents, Excel spreadsheets, PowerPoint presentations, OneNote meeting notes, Publisher publications, and Outlook e-mail—with voice and unified communications services such as Click-to-Call, Presence, Instant Messaging, voice and videoconferencing, and desktop sharing gives users a powerful and innovative communications platform.

One of the newest members of the Microsoft Office suite is Microsoft Office Communicator. This application, now in its 2007 R2 release, as explained earlier in the book, provides the information worker with a stellar Instant Messaging, voice, and videoconferencing solution packaged into one application. With Communicator running on the desktop, other Microsoft applications such as Microsoft Office Outlook are lit up with the Communicator Presence indicator lights indicating a contact's availability or presence in or out of the office (see Figure 6.1).

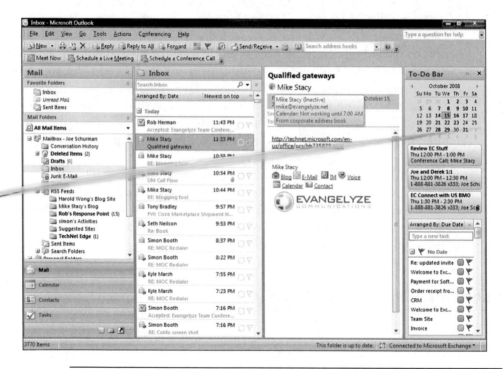

**FIGURE 6.1** Presence status indicator in Microsoft Office Outlook

Let's say you just received a note about a contract and you had questions about it. You notice that the person or group that sent you the contract via e-mail is available by looking at the green status indicator adjacent to their name. You can, directly from the e-mail, click on the contact's name and start an Instant Messaging, voice, or video conversation in seconds. Need the whole group? You can drag and drop other contacts directly into your conversation, and you're all instantly communicating. Now that's productivity that is a soft cost return on investment that is instantly realized. In Chapter 9, "How to Sell Voice and Unified Communications," I discuss how to quickly enable a Microsoft partner to sell this technology. Part of the UC 1-2-3 sales methodology that I present has to do with quickly enabling a customer in a pilot engagement to immediately see the benefits of integration like this by leveraging preconfigured virtual server environments running Microsoft Office and the Microsoft Unified Communications platform together so that this kind of innovation—that WOW effect—is immediately experienced by the customer.

Let's take this a step further. Let's say you've shut down Outlook because you're concentrating on a presentation, document, or spreadsheet and don't want to be bothered. What's awesome is that if you are working on a document that has another contact listed or named within the document and that contact exists in your Communicator contacts list, you can directly communicate, as described in the previous scenario with Outlook, directly from Word, Excel, and PowerPoint. Again, WOW!

Figures 6.2, 6.3, and 6.4 show the Presence status indicator of a contact directly from within Microsoft Office Word, Excel, and PowerPoint.

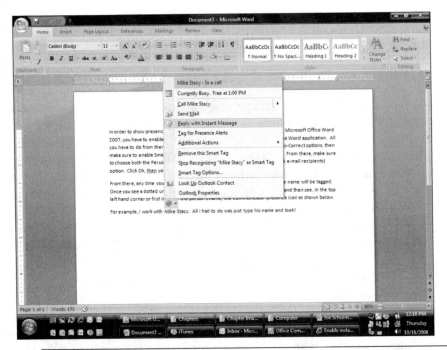

**FIGURE 6.2** UC Presence in Microsoft Office Word

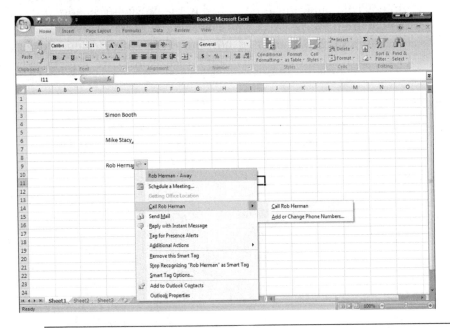

**FIGURE 6.3** UC Presence in Microsoft Office Excel

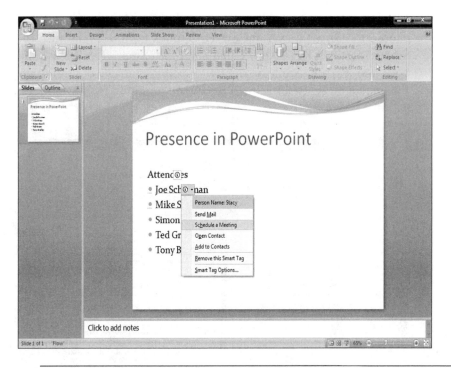

**FIGURE 6.4** UC Presence in Microsoft Office PowerPoint

Smart Tags are not enabled by default, but enabling them is easy. All you have to do is click on the Tools menu in Office 2003 or the Office icon in the top left-hand corner of Office 2007 and choose the Word or Excel options menu as shown in Figure 6.5 using Microsoft Office Word 2007.

From there, choose the Proofing action in the menu on the left, and choose the Smart Tag AutoCorrect Options button. Make sure to enable Smart Tags by selecting the Label Data with Smart Tags option and select both the Person Name (English or your language of preference) and Person Name (Outlook E-mail Recipients) options as shown in Figure 6.6 within Microsoft Office Word 2007.

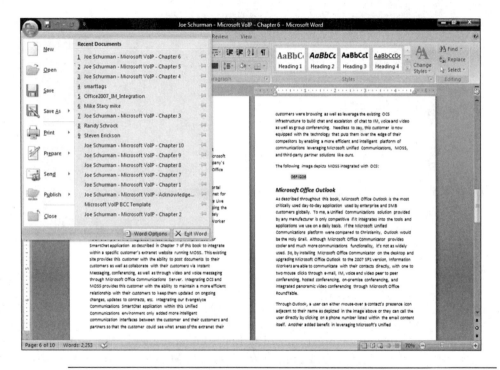

**FIGURE 6.5** Microsoft Office Word 2007 Word Options menu

**FIGURE 6.6** Enabling Smart Tags

You can see how easy it is to extend presence and voice communication throughout the Microsoft Office suite increasing productivity on a daily basis.

# Microsoft Office SharePoint Server

Extending presence and messaging capabilities to Microsoft's most popular server product outside Windows Server with Microsoft Office SharePoint Server (MOSS) is only a natural progression for the company's innovative look at integrating Unified Communications across the Office suite.

To me, Unified Communications is incomplete without tie-ins to portal applications such as MOSS. Being able to browse the extranet or intranet for specific documents, record conferences through Microsoft Office Live Meeting and Microsoft Office RoundTable, and then ping the contact or group associated with the content rounds out a completely unified application platform and duly increases daily information worker productivity tenfold.

As an example of this integrated functionality, my firm provided our SmartChat application as described in Chapter 7, "Customizing Voice Applications," to integrate within a specific customer's extranet Web site running MOSS. This existing site provides this customer the ability to post documents to their customers as well as collaborate with their customers via Instant Messaging, conferencing, and video and voice messaging through Microsoft Office Communications Server. Integrating OCS and MOSS provides this customer the ability to maintain a more efficient relationship with their customers to keep them informed on ongoing changes, updates to contracts, and so on (see Figure 6.7). Integrating our Evangelyze Communications SmartChat application within this Unified Communications environment adds more intelligent communication interfaces between the customer and their customers and partners so that the customer could see what areas of the extranet their customers were browsing as well as leverage the existing OCS infrastructure to build chat and escalation of chat to IM, voice, and video as well as group conferencing. Needless to say, this customer is now equipped with the technology that puts them over the edge of their competitors by enabling a more efficient and intelligent platform of communications leveraging Microsoft Unified Communications, MOSS, and third-party partner solutions like ours.

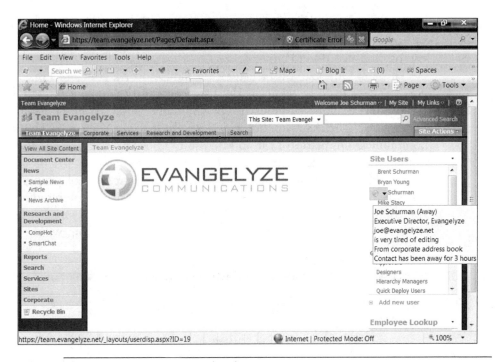

**FIGURE 6.7** MOSS integrated with OCS

# Microsoft Office Outlook

As described throughout this book, Microsoft Office Outlook is the most critical day-to-day application used by enterprise and SMB customers globally. A Unified Communications solution provided by any manufacturer is only competitive if it integrates into the tools and applications we use on a daily basis. If the Microsoft Unified Communications platform were compared to Christianity, Outlook would be the Holy Grail. Although Microsoft Office Communicator provides much more (and cooler) communications functionality, it's not as widely used. So, by installing Microsoft Office Communicator on the desktop and upgrading Microsoft Office Outlook to the 2007 SP1 version, information workers can communicate with contacts directly, with one to two mouse clicks through e-mail, IM,

voice and video peer-to-peer conferencing, hosted conferencing, on-premise conferencing, and integrated panoramic videoconferencing through Microsoft Office RoundTable.

Through Outlook, a user can either mouse over a contact's Presence icon adjacent to their name or the user can call the contact directly by clicking on a phone number listed within the e-mail content itself as depicted in Figure 6.8. Another added benefit in using Microsoft's Unified Communications platform within Microsoft Office Outlook is access to the Unified Messaging features of Microsoft Exchange Server 2007. In addition to adding a separate tab for Voice Mail inside your Outlook properties dialog box, the user can see missed call notification e-mails generated from Microsoft Exchange Server (see Figure 6.9) as well as voicemail e-mail notifications as well (see Figure 6.10), playable directly from within the Outlook application.

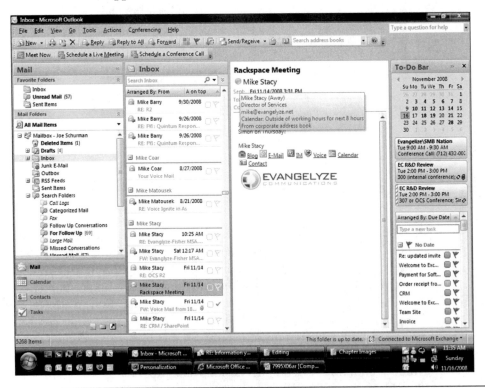

**FIGURE 6.8** Presence availability within Microsoft Office Outlook

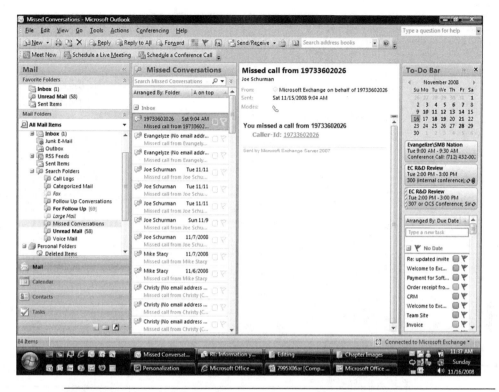

**FIGURE 6.9** Missed Call Notifications in Microsoft Office Outlook

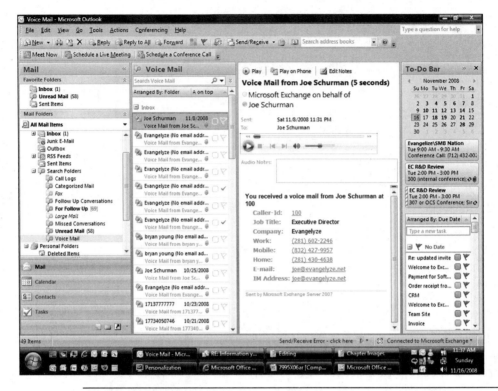

**FIGURE 6.10** Voicemail messages in Microsoft Office Outlook

To add, this same functionality is made available to users via Windows Mobile, BlackBerry, and, my favorite mobile app at the moment, Microsoft Exchange for the Apple iPhone.

When I'm working out at the gym or out and about, I can be listening to music on my iPhone, browsing some of the cool iPhone apps, whatever. If I miss a call that comes in on my company line that I have set up using simultaneous ring to my mobile, I receive a push e-mail notification showing the missed call number, which I can click to call directly from the iPhone mail application as well as play the embedded voicemail as well (see Figure 6.11). Now that is brilliant!

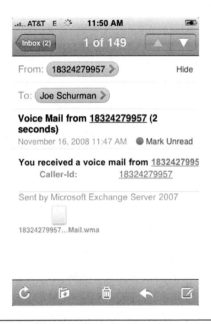

**FIGURE 6.11** iPhone Missed Call and Voicemail notifications

To enable voicemail and e-mail integration to your Outlook account, you must complete the following actions:

1. Make sure that your organization is running Microsoft Exchange Server 2007 with Service Pack 1 and has the Unified Messaging module installed and configured.
2. For Click-to-Call functionality within Outlook on the PC, make sure your organization has at least Microsoft Office Communications Server 2007 or version R2 installed and configured.
3. The phone number or extension assigned your account must be linked and configured inside OCS and Exchange as well as Active Directory.
4. You must be running Microsoft Office 2007 with Service Pack 1.
5. Within the Voice Mail tab of your Microsoft Office Outlook application, you should see these properties already assigned as shown by example in Figure 6.12.
6. To have your mobile number simultaneously ring when someone calls your corporate extension, you must set this property within Microsoft Office Communicator as shown in Figure 6.13.

6. VOICE COLLABORATION

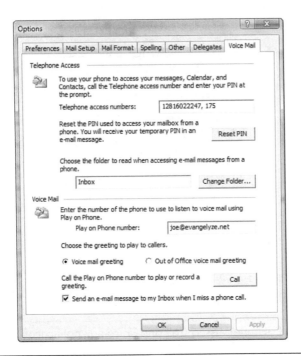

**FIGURE 6.12** Voicemail tab in Microsoft Office Outlook

7. From there, you just need to use a Windows Mobile device running 6.0 or later or the iPhone running version 2.0 or later, and you're good to go.

Another powerful Outlook add-in has to do with conferencing. You now have the capability using either Hosted Live Meeting services online or Live Meeting running as the Conferencing control unit within Microsoft Office Communications Server for on-premise meetings, both integrated with cool devices like the Microsoft Office RoundTable device, to start a conference directly from within Microsoft Outlook. Using the Live Meeting Add-In for Outlook 2007, you can schedule a meeting in the future or use the Meet Now feature to start a conference on the spot. The beauty of Live Meeting is that you can use computer audio and video as well as VoIP and PSTN call integration to enable the most innovative conferencing tool in the market, again, directly from Microsoft Office Outlook.

**FIGURE 6.13** Simultaneous Ring setting in Communicator

Figure 6.14 depicts the Microsoft Office Live Meeting add-in toolbar for Microsoft Office Outlook 2007 with SP1.

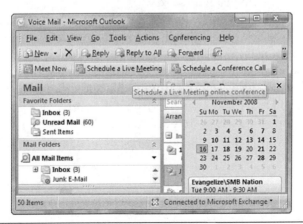

**FIGURE 6.14** Live Meeting Add-In toolbar for Outlook 2007 SP1

Hopefully, you get the picture now. From within Outlook on the PC, Mac OS X, Windows Mobile, iPhone, BlackBerry, and soon the Web, you can use Outlook to serve as the foundation for all modes of communication using the Microsoft Unified Communications platform. Just so you know, the only competitor to Microsoft in this space would be IBM, but IBM falls short in that they do not provide the software-based PBX features that Office Communications Server does, so it's really an incomplete Unified Communications solution. However, the IBM Lotus suite of office products does now include presence, messaging, and conferencing functionality. In summary, it's clear to see how Microsoft provides a true end-to-end Unified Communications platform and information worker story improving day-to-day productivity.

## Microsoft Unified Communications and Microsoft Office "Better Together" Videos

The information in this chapter is a good overview of what is available in regards to integrating the Microsoft Unified Communications platform with the Microsoft Office suite of applications. As a guy in his early thirties, it's much easier for me to understand things visually. To this effect, Microsoft has created a ton of cool, scenario-based videos that we have received permission to place on the resource Web site via http://www.schurman.name/microsoftvoice.asp, referenced in Appendix A, "Closing Comments and Resources." For an online view of these videos, simply go to YouTube, MSN, or Google Video and search for "Microsoft Unified Communications satire."

These videos visually help you understand how the technology is used. You can see how much detail Microsoft went into in regards to hiring the actors, production studios, and so on. It's definitely worth a look! So far, the most popular satire video is the UC satire on the movie *The Devil Wears Prada*, which was removed from publication due to copyright issues with the actual Hollywood movie. Fortunately, everyone who has seen or downloaded the video has posted the movie all over the Web!

# CHAPTER 7

# CUSTOMIZING VOICE APPLICATIONS

Outside of integrating the Microsoft Unified Communications platform with the Microsoft Office suite, the most competitive feature of Microsoft's Unified Communications solution versus other competitors is the open platform for third-party application development and integration made available through Microsoft Visual Studio and other development tools.

Many other competitors lock down their Unified Communications applications, forcing customers to use only their tools, making the end user open yet another application on the desktop, and by not integrating these services into applications that end users leverage on a daily basis, such as the Microsoft Office suite.

This chapter outlines what integration functionality is available with the Microsoft Unified Communications platform.

## Microsoft Office Communications Server Customization

As mentioned in Chapter 4, "Enterprise Voice with Microsoft Unified Communications," Microsoft Office Communications Server (OCS) is Microsoft's software-powered PBX system. Evolving from Microsoft Office Live Communications Server 2003 to today's 2007 R2 version, OCS provides the following areas of customization for developers:

- n Office Communications Server 2007 Software Developer Kit (SDK)
- n Unified Communications Managed API (UCMA)
- n Office Communications Server 2007 Speech Server API

## Office Communications Server 2007 SDK

The OCS 2007 SDK provides an API developer kit for two levels of extensibility for Microsoft OCS focused on server application and server management extensibility. The SDK allows developers to extend the features of OCS leveraging Microsoft SIP Processing Language (MSSPL) or develop enhanced management tools using Windows Management Instrumentation (WMI) for Windows Server. Both APIs provide a ton of flexibility for developers who want to create specific niche applications to sell as third-party partner applications or to develop customized solutions that fit a specific line of business needs for their organizations.

### OCS Server Application API

Using the OCS Server Application API, developers can develop SIP messaging and routing solutions as well as leverage the OCS SIP developer Manifest. Using this API, and tools like Microsoft Visual Studio, currently in its 2008 release with C# or Visual Basic, developers can create and integrate some cool apps. I have found that many developers build on the templates published via the MSDN Unified Communications portal and complete their solutions from this development boost rather than starting from scratch. Other developers, such as my colleague and director of research and development at Evangelyze Communications (EC), Simon Booth, love starting from scratch, enabling Simon to customize and create some of the coolest OCS applications on the planet.

For more information on the OCS Server Application API, visit http://msdn.microsoft.com/en-us/library/bb632196.aspx.

### OCS Server Management API

Using the OCS Server Management API, developers can create more IT administrator-focused applications to handle management tasks such as migrating users from competitive platforms, directories, and so on or adding enhanced WMI management classes to customize the management of OCS server properties.

An example of using the OCS Server Management API was written by colleagues and fellow consultants of mine for a Lotus Notes migration project that we provided for a noncustomer approved reference engagement. This multibillion dollar financial services organization had many thousands of users within its Lotus Domino directory that needed to be migrated to Microsoft OCS, which requires Microsoft Active Directory. At the time, and there's still nothing really wonderful in the market today that handles this problem, there was not any way to automate the importing of bulk amounts of users into the new Microsoft system to enable these users for Microsoft Unified Communications. Through the OCS Server Management API, my colleagues created a solution using WMI to auto-export and import a bulk directory of contacts into Microsoft Active Directory and then automate the enabling of each contact for basic Instant Messaging functionality. From there, only select users were enabled for Voice so this tool handled the bulk load of users.

For more information on the OCS Server Management API, visit http://msdn.microsoft.com/en-us/library/bb632198.aspx.

## Unified Communications Managed API SDK

The UCMA is used by .NET developers to create similar services provided by Microsoft OCS itself. Essentially a SIP stack, this server or client API allows developers to create server or middle-tier applications to control the content of SIP messages for video, voice, and data/conferencing control for those who really seek a customized Unified Communications solution, aka, those who "think outside the box."

An example of why a developer would want to use the UCMA would be to develop a SIP Server that can handle highly scalable transactions outside the normal behavior of Microsoft OCS, which, bear in mind, is extreme, or because of issues where corporate or military stringent security requirements prevent the use of OCS's out-of-the-box functionality.

A real world example of using the UCMA SDK has been developed by my colleague, Simon Booth. Simon has developed several highly innovative Microsoft Unified Communications custom development applications that have blown even Microsoft away. One of these applications, named SmartConference, is a Web-based scheduling tool that leverages the UCMA to schedule on-premise Live Meeting conferences and voice conference calls within Microsoft OCS. For some reason the Microsoft development team left this solution out of the packaged product offering of OCS 2007, so Simon, based on a global need for this solution, took it upon himself to develop this missing product. Using the UCMA, Simon created a sleek UI that ties into OCS to create, edit, and manage meetings and conferences as well as integrates with Exchange Server and Outlook to synchronize scheduled meetings to an end user's or group's calendar.

Figure 7.1 is a screen shot of the EC SmartConference application.

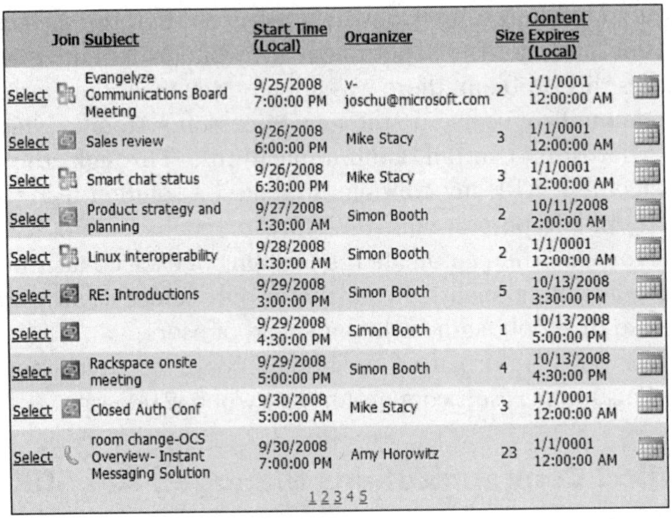

| Join | Subject | Start Time (Local) | Organizer | Size | Content Expires (Local) | |
|---|---|---|---|---|---|---|
| Select | Evangelyze Communications Board Meeting | 9/25/2008 7:00:00 PM | v-joschu@microsoft.com | 2 | 1/1/0001 12:00:00 AM | |
| Select | Sales review | 9/26/2008 6:00:00 PM | Mike Stacy | 3 | 1/1/0001 12:00:00 AM | |
| Select | Smart chat status | 9/26/2008 6:30:00 PM | Mike Stacy | 3 | 1/1/0001 12:00:00 AM | |
| Select | Product strategy and planning | 9/27/2008 1:30:00 AM | Simon Booth | 2 | 10/11/2008 2:00:00 AM | |
| Select | Linux interoperability | 9/28/2008 1:30:00 AM | Simon Booth | 2 | 1/1/0001 12:00:00 AM | |
| Select | RE: Introductions | 9/29/2008 3:00:00 PM | Simon Booth | 5 | 10/13/2008 3:30:00 PM | |
| Select | | 9/29/2008 4:30:00 PM | Simon Booth | 1 | 10/13/2008 5:00:00 PM | |
| Select | Rackspace onsite meeting | 9/29/2008 5:00:00 PM | Simon Booth | 4 | 10/13/2008 4:30:00 PM | |
| Select | Closed Auth Conf | 9/30/2008 5:00:00 AM | Mike Stacy | 3 | 1/1/0001 12:00:00 AM | |
| Select | room change-OCS Overview- Instant Messaging Solution | 9/30/2008 7:00:00 PM | Amy Horowitz | 23 | 1/1/0001 12:00:00 AM | |

1 2 3 4 5

**FIGURE 7.1** SmartConference Beta 1

## Unified Communications Bots

The UCMA SDK is also widely used for bot development. **Bots,** short for ro**Bots,** are applications created to serve as response solutions within Microsoft OCS. UC Bots are like simulated Communicator users in the system. They have accounts created within Microsoft Active Directory or leverage a separate AD login and account to automatically sign in to Microsoft OCS as a user. Once online, these bots or resources can be communicated with by primarily using Instant Messaging, but bots are being developed to test video and audio as well as telephony communication. Bots are great resources as well, and I have seen Microsoft and other developers create bots for resources such as Expedia. Imagine a Wikipedia, Google, or Windows Live Search bot that you could use to type a keyword, for example "Unified Communications," and have the bot respond with information and links to additional resources. Take the development a step further to create bots that respond to commands and then they initiate other applications or processes inside the organization, and now you're thinkin'! Needless to say, there is definitely a market for UC bots today.

As an example, we use a UC bot to respond to customer or external contact requests using our EC SmartChat solution. This bot responds to general questions and welcomes the contact on the initiating chat session as shown in Figure 7.2.

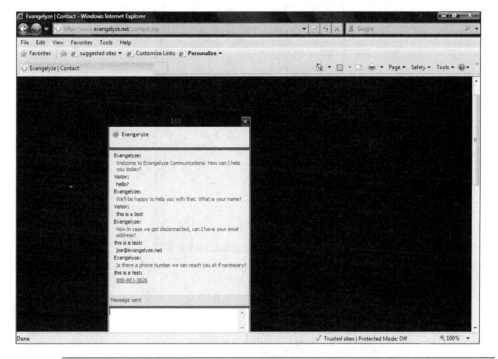

**FIGURE 7.2** SmartChat Instant Messaging screen

This bot is a registered OCS contact and shows up in our contact list as the Anonymous Web User contact as shown in Figure 7.3.

**FIGURE 7.3** UC bot as a contact

During the chat session, the customer interfaces with us through the Web using the SmartChat application, but on our side, we use Microsoft Office Communicator with a custom developed screen showing us the activity and/or Microsoft CRM record for this contact as shown in Figure 7.4.

For more information on UC bot development using the UCMA SDK, visit http://unified-communications-development.blogspot.com/ search?q=ucma and look at the Friday, May 23, 2008 entry entitled, "sing UCMA to create a custom routing bot!".

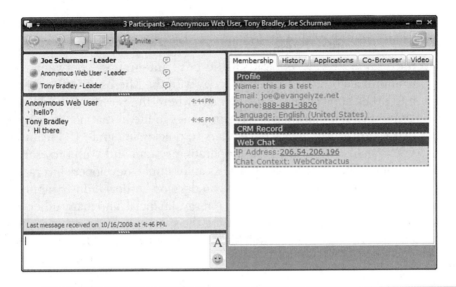

**FIGURE 7.4** SmartChat extension for Microsoft Office Communicator

Currently, the UCMA SDK supports at Windows Server 2003 and Windows Server 2008 with Hyper-V as well. The UCMA is written in Microsoft C#, which can be viewed as a limitation to some developers, but C# is viewed as a solid development language by the development community at large.

For more information on the UCMA SDK and API, visit http://msdn.microsoft.com/en-us/library/bb773159.aspx.

## Microsoft Office Communicator Customization

Customizing Communicator is kind of misleading. The actual Microsoft Office Communicator application is locked down with the exception of extending the Communicator tab interface and within the Actions menu off the Communicator application, unless you create your own customized client using the Unified Communications Client API. Otherwise, leveraging the Office Communicator Automation API allows developers to extend the features and functionality of Communicator into custom or line of business applications, all of which are described in more detail over the following sections with specific examples.

## Office Communicator Automation API

Using the Office Communicator Automation API, developers can build the same level of out-of-the-box integration between Office Communicator 2007 that exists today with the Microsoft Office 2007 suite into other applications. This is really where the power of the Microsoft's Unified Communications platform comes to life in that no other competitive UC platform allows developers to quickly integrate UC features and functionality within their own, operating system and Web browser agnostic, line of business applications. As an example, developers leveraging the Communicator Automation API can develop vertical industry applications for industries such as healthcare, energy, financial, and many others so that business users who are used to using the specific and mostly non-Microsoft line of business apps, can quickly integrate voice, video, Instant Messaging, presence, and conferencing directly into these applications with very little code.

A great example of using the Microsoft Office Communicator Automation API was written by Simon as well. Simon used the API to develop screen pops and integration between Office Communicator functionality within a popular customer relationship management application, Microsoft CRM.

As shown in the previous "Unified Communications Bots" section, we are able to extend the Communicator client to enable CRM integration. Figure 7.5 shows how we can further extend the client to add additional functionality such as reviewing the pages a contact has viewed via his Web browser as well as other information that may be useful during a chat session. Another cool extension of this solution is by enabling Call Back to allow us to dial the contact back using VoIP through Microsoft Office Communicator or by making the chat more personal by showing video as depicted in Figure 7.5.

Although this is another Microsoft application, the same level of integration can be applied to non-Microsoft applications leveraging the presence and communication Task menu built into Microsoft Office Communicator, to register and integrate into the line of business application wherever a contact or group's name is displayed.

For more information regarding the Microsoft Office Communicator Automation API, visit http://msdn.microsoft.com/enus/library/bb758719.aspx.

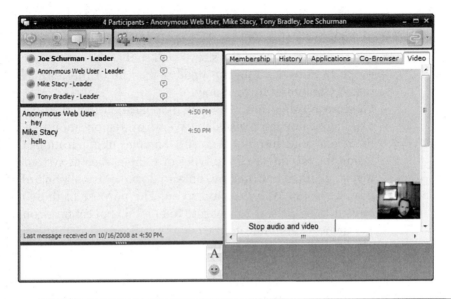

**FIGURE 7.5** SmartChat audio/video window

## Microsoft Office Communicator Tabs

Tab-based extensibility has been around since the Communicator 2005 release. Tabs are really only an extra portion of the Communicator menu as the Communicator application itself is pretty locked down. The tab extension is an XML-driven application interface that displays whatever the developer creates via a Web page or Web-based application. The Communicator application calls the XML descriptor file for which the developer provides the following information for the application to display properly:

n **Icon/logo**. The logo or icon is displayed at the bottom part of the default Microsoft Office Communicator application. Once clicked on, the logo launches the tab interface where the tab-based application is loaded. This logo file is usually loaded on a Web or file server widely available to end users running Microsoft Office Communicator so that security permissions or other issues would prevent the image from showing. Note that the icon image only displays if there is more than one tab.

n **XML descriptor file**. This file is used to define the link to the actual application that will be displayed within the Communicator tab and the dimensions of the site as well so that the application can be properly viewed within the small real estate of the normally minimized Communicator window.

n **Custom application**. The actual application that runs within the Communicator tab is usually a Web-based application that resides on a company's intranet Web site. Samples of applications that run inside the tab interface are types of utilities such as system reporting, stock price information, links to documents on a SharePoint or intranet portal Web site, and so on. The purpose of these applications is to help users to navigate to helpful applications from within the same Communicator window to eliminate multiple windows running on the desktop, thereby creating a utility toolbelt within Communicator.

As another real world example, my company, Evangelyze Communications (EC), has developed a simple Redial option for Microsoft Office Communicator. We use the tab feature to extend the Redial option as shown in Figure 7.6.

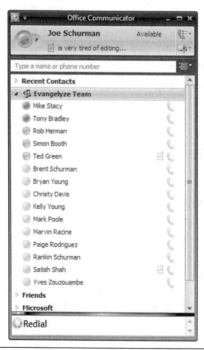

**FIGURE 7.6** EC Redial button for Microsoft Office Communicator

For more information on how to create tab-based applications for Microsoft Office Communicator, visit http://www.microsoft.com/ downloads/ and search for "Communicator tabs." There you can download sample tab applications as well.

## Unified Communications Client SDK

The ultimate client SDK for developing customized Unified Communications end-user applications is the UC Client SDK. This COM-based API enables developers to create customized UC client applications that can leverage all the features of Microsoft Office Communicator and extend features and functionality created by the developer for specific business needs or just for a "coolness" factor.

As an example, Microsoft Office Communicator itself is built using the Unified Communications Client SDK. With this SDK, Microsoft really put the power in the hands of the people, the developers, who can create a wide range of communication and collaboration applications, enabling the development of some of the most innovative cross-industry or industry-specific applications in the world.

For more information regarding the Microsoft UC Client SDK, visit http://msdn.microsoft.com/en-us/library/bb878684.aspx.

## Unified Communications AJAX SDK

The Unified Communications Asynchronous JavaScript and XML (AJAX) SDK is one of my favorite development platforms in that a developer can quickly create platform and Web browser agnostic applications that leverage the Microsoft Unified Communications client features of Microsoft Office Communicator, but also provide the flexibility of creating some really stellar customer Web applications.

AJAX is an XML-based programming language that has become popular since 2005 and is now widely used to create Web-based applications for enterprise and SMB organizations as well as for social networking and customer-focused Web sites. The beauty of AJAX is that this coding language can be used to create applications that can run on any operating system or through any Web browser, extending the reach of the application to many end users.

As an example of this innovation, Simon created another product that we sell at EC called SmartChat.

EC SmartChat is a solution that allows organizations to leverage their investment in OCS 2007 to provide a real-time Web-based chat solution for external and/or internal customers. Powered by rich presence, SmartChat allows for multiple routing options for complete flexibility, including rules such as

- Group membership
- Hierarchical escalation
- User properties
- Location/Time of day
- Web site context
- Contact list membership
- Round robin
- Shifts or queue duration
- Bot escalation
- Custom business rules

SmartChat extends the existing OCS Presence engine to automatically indicate whether agents are available for a chat session. If a customer accesses the system outside service hours the site automatically updates to send an e-mail or perform other actions. The SmartChat user interface operates within any Internet, extranet, or intranet environment and has been tested with Internet Explorer 6, 7, and 8; Firefox 2 and 3; Google Chrome beta; and Safari 3. SmartChat requires no additional software installation for either the customer or the agent.

Figure 7.7 depicts the EC SmartChat application that leverages Unified Communications.

Because of the available language packs, we are also able to extend SmartChat in any supported language, globally as depicted in Figures 7.8 and 7.9.

**FIGURE 7.7** SmartChat application (running on EC Web site)

**FIGURE 7.8** SmartChat in Dutch

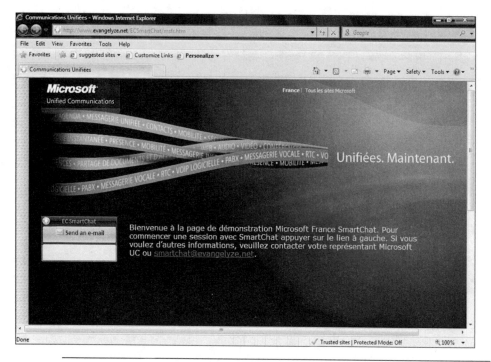

**FIGURE 7.9** SmartChat in French

By leveraging the UC AJAX API, Simon developed a solution that was missing from the Microsoft Unified Communications platform and aided the brand awareness of our organization in that we provided a solution that our customers need to leverage within their organizations and to build better insight and relationships with their partners and customers.

For more information on the Unified Communications AJAX SDK and API, visit http://msdn.microsoft.com/en-us/library/bb969621.aspx.

## Microsoft Office Live Meeting Customization

As described in Chapter 4, Microsoft Office Live Meeting is available in two models: hosted and on-premise. The Live Meeting hosted solution is hosted by Microsoft or other hosting providers and end users schedule and host meetings online. The Live Meeting on-premise solution is part of the Microsoft OCS architecture as a separate module called the Conferencing Multipoint Control Unit (MCU). Customization options are available today for developers for both the hosted and on-premise models using the Microsoft Office Live Meeting Service API as described in the following sections.

## Live Meeting Portal API

End users are invited to a Live Meeting conference using either the Live Meeting hosted service—these users log in to a Live Meeting client—or a browser-based client. Both solutions take the user to the hosted Live Meeting service and within the service lies the hosted Live Meeting Portal, which hosts the Live Meeting conference and enables a Web-based lobby as well for participants to sit and wait until the conference begins, if enabled by the presenter for that specific meeting.

The Live Meeting Service Portal API is used by developers to customize the look and feel of the portal pages such as the welcome page for each type of participant of the meeting be it the administrator, organizer, or conference joining member/attendee. A developer can use the SDK to edit these pages within a Web design tool such as DreamWeaver, Expression Web, or other Web design applications to edit these pages to their liking.

Figure 7.10 depicts a customized Live Meeting Portal welcome page provided by Microsoft for Microsoft Unified Communications MVPs.

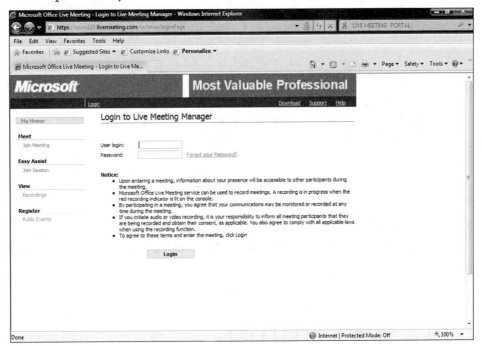

**Figure 7.10** Microsoft Office Live Meeting Portal for Microsoft MVPs

A more advanced use of the Live Meeting Portal API by developers is the automation of user account creation, sign-on, deletion of users, and account status and activation. This is important because some Microsoft Unified Communications customers want to use the hosted Microsoft Live Meeting service for all their conferences, or use the service for all their customer or partner-facing conferences and use the on-premise conferencing for Live Meeting within OCS for internal or private meetings. By using the Live Meeting Portal API, developers can automate the account creation of bulk amounts of users or individual users as well as the updating or removal/deletion of these user accounts as these accounts lie within a separate, hosted directory, not managed by the customer's internal Microsoft Active Directory using Lightweight Directory Access Protocol (LDAP) and XML programming. Some of these tools have already been written and are available for purchase online so that the customer's internal developers do not have to re-create the process.

For more information on the Live Meeting Portal API, visit http://msdn.microsoft.com/en-us/library/bb969445.aspx. For more information on customizing the Live Meeting Portal pages, visit http://msdn.microsoft.com/en-us/library/bb969461.aspx.

# Microsoft Exchange Server Customization

An entire book can be and has been written on Microsoft Exchange Server custom development, so I do not try to replicate this information. The purpose of this book is to cover VoIP and Unified Communications topics, so the focus of this section covers only how to use the Microsoft Exchange Server 2007 SP1 SDK for customized development solutions as they relate to Unified Messaging and Unified Communications. To this effect, this section concentrates more on Exchange Web Services and introduces a not so well-known solution for Exchange Server 2007 Unified Messaging as described in the following sections.

## Exchange Web Services for Unified Communications

Microsoft Exchange Web Services is one of the most innovative development services ever created by Microsoft. Eliminating roadblocks and other complexities caused by programming tools such as WebDAV, CDOEX, and others, Exchange Web Services leverages cross-platform programming languages and standards to achieve customization and integration of Exchange features and functionality through the following technologies:

- n Hypertext Transport Protocol (HTTP)
- n eXtensible Markup Language (XML)
- n Simple Object Access Protocol (SOAP)
- n Web Services Description Language (WSDL)

In the world of Unified Communications, Exchange Web Services can be used to integrate video, voice, and data conference meetings with scheduling services provided by Microsoft Exchange Server to schedule meetings in the calendar for rooms, groups, and individuals and by synchronizing these meetings with mobile devices and PCs running Outlook Mobile and Outlook for the PC as well as Mac OS X computers running Microsoft Office 2008 and Web-based calendaring software such as Outlook Web Access. Leveraging this extensive code base, developers can write scheduling applications that cross multiple operating systems and Web browsers to enable end users with a truly unified solution for messaging, collaboration, and voice communications.

An example of an application developed for leveraging Exchange Web Services is SmartConference, the same application mentioned earlier in this chapter regarding the UCMA. The SmartConference application connects to an organization's Microsoft OCS to create voice, video, and Live Meeting conferences and then uses Exchange Web Services for scheduling and synchronization of the meetings within the conference organizer's and conference participant's calendar.

Earlier in Figure 7.1, a user can see a list of calendar items within the EC SmartConference application. Figure 7.11 is a screen shot of the EC SmartConference application when a user opens a specific event, which enables the user to send to other possible meeting participants or simply synchronize with their Microsoft Office Outlook calendar.

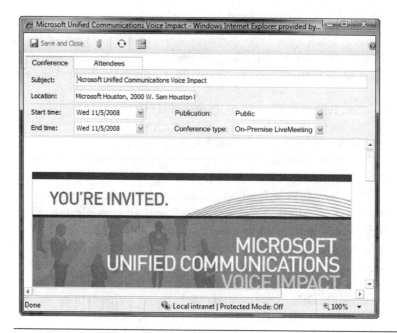

**FIGURE 7.11** SmartConference Event using Exchange Web Services

Another cool feature of this application that is also missing today from OCS is the ability for an external participant to join an on-premise meeting and confirm their attendance over the Web. The EC SmartConference application allows for external parties, cross-firewall, to join and confirm a voice, video, or data conference directly over the Web for OCS on-premise conferences. Now that is innovation provided by the yet ever extendable Unified Communications development platform.

For a detailed overview of Exchange Web Services, visit http://msdn.microsoft.com/en-us/library/bb408417.aspx.

## Exchange Server Unified Messaging Web Service

A somewhat unknown and lightly documented development API for the Microsoft Exchange Server Unified Messaging component, the Exchange Server Unified Messaging Web Service provides developers with the ability to leverage the Exchange Unified Messaging component, which is a Web service itself for scenarios such as manipulating the PlayMessagesonPhone method or retrieving a list of MessageIDs with Caller ID information for other uses such as reporting or automation.

This is really an area that has been untapped and could possibly be used to transfer copies of voicemail messages, message detail, or other important call information to multiple applications and devices. Little information is known about this subject at the time, but I encourage you to play around with the UM Web service and hopefully come up with a development scenario that has some kind of business value or coolness factor to help build a community of sample applications. Until then, you can view more information on the Exchange Server Unified Messaging Web Service via http://msdn.microsoft.com/en-us/library/cc540447(EXCHG.80).aspx.

In summary, there are many, many more capabilities to extend Microsoft Exchange Server and even leverage Microsoft Office SDKs and APIs to extend the capabilities of Microsoft Office Outlook to enable the development of some cool Unified Communications and Unified Messaging enabled applications.

For more information on development solutions and extending features of Microsoft Exchange Server visit http://msdn.microsoft.com/en-us/library/bb418718(EXCHG.80).aspx. For an overview of the Microsoft Exchange Server 2007 SP1 SDK visit http://msdn.microsoft.com/en-us/library/aa562613(EXCHG.80).aspx.

# Custom Speech Development

A new area of custom development in the Unified Communications space is actually not so new for the existing Speech Server gurus out there. As mentioned earlier in this book, Microsoft Speech Server is now part of the Microsoft Unified Communications platform as well as Microsoft Response Point and serves a primary role now with Auto-Attendant features and voice command operations in both solutions. One of the most innovative solutions provided by the former Microsoft Speech Server team was the Speech Server SDK. Using the SDK and available APIs as well as a series of templates and sample projects for the Microsoft Visual Studio .NET suite, developers can now create custom call workflows and also develop new custom voice command/speech services for their own applications.

Microsoft uses this technology to benefit products such as Outlook Voice Access and the Exchange Server Unified Messaging solution with the Exchange Auto-Attendant as well as the built-in speech recognition features of Microsoft Response Point. Speech customization and automation have been around for some time, but we are just now on the cusp of enhancements that will change the way we communicate forever.

For more detailed information on the Speech SDK, APIs, and developer kits for Visual Studio .NET, visit http://msdn.microsoft.com/en-us/library/bb857803.aspx.

## Developer Resources

Today there are many opportunities for developers to customize Microsoft Unified Communications solutions, and the best starting point for accelerating this activity is through the thorough and popular MSDN (Microsoft Developer Network) portal for Microsoft Unified Communications, accessible online via http://msdn.microsoft.com/en-us/office/aa905374.aspx. Through this Web site, developers can download sample code, review server architecture, leverage API templates, and much more.

In summary, extending the Unified Communications platform by making APIs and SDK kits available to developers is the most innovative and the smartest choice Microsoft has made, which will keep them at the top of the list of competitive Unified Communications solutions in the marketplace. So for you developers or IT pros whom I have struck a chord with in this chapter, start building your customized UC application today and Happy Coding!

# CHAPTER 8

# SECURING VOICE

We made it through the Y2K scare. We are now all accustomed to antivirus software, bad Web sites, phishing, and the many nasty security breaches that put user data at risk. Most annoying, we are all familiar with the daily plague called SPAM. Now, our organizations and personal data must confront new security challenges such as SPIM, messaging overflows, tapping, and other threats that can instantly disrupt and/or compromise the security of personal and corporate information.

Traditionally, voice networks and data networks have been entirely separate. While the convergence of the two into digital voice and unified communications delivers a variety of cost and feature benefits, it also opens up the voice network to many of the risks and threats that previously only impacted data networks. Converting voice data to IP packets and sending it over the data network means exposing it to new attacks.

In this chapter, we identify some of the new threats we are currently seeing today in voice and unified communications products and services and discuss how to easily prevent these by applying standards-based security applications and by using newly introduced security products.

## Voice and UC Security Threats

Security, unfortunately, is frequently reactive. Hackers will always find a way through network defenses to your personal or corporate data. Software and hardware manufacturers will always provide a fix for this behavior. This cyclical process has been happening since the first network was created and has been amplified by the past decade of millions of users signing in each day to a worldwide network of computers and applications.

Throughout this book, I have outlined innovations in voice communications to reduce costs and improve flexibility in the way we communicate by presenting small business, enterprise, and consumer voice and unified communications solutions from Microsoft. These innovative products and services provide the future of voice communications. Today, you are more than likely familiar with products such as Skype, Asterisk, Vonage, and other virtualized SIP-enabled phone systems, all of which have the same goal of reducing the cost of voice communications from traditional Telcos and wireless carriers. The only problem with this is that we are now taking voice communications to a Web-based communications platform, prone to hacking, tapping or listening, spoofing, and, more dangerously, invading.

The only real threat that we know of today with traditional voice communications is tapping of the line as approved and exposed most recently in the Patriot Act legislation passed shortly after the 9/11 terrorist attacks on the United States. As more companies and consumers start adopting and using voice and unified communications technology, more serious security attacks are available now for hackers to expose or use to provide a detriment to you or your organization. The following are the top three most common threats to these communications services:

- **SPAM for Instant Messaging (SPIM)**. An evolution of our most-loved daily ritual of deleting and removing of unwanted e-mail messages called SPAM, SPIM is a new version of SPAM used for the sole purpose of annoying Instant Messaging users. Outside sending unwanted and annoying IM messages, SPIM can quickly be programmed to create an overflow of messages enabling a buffer overflow (overflow of data) on IM servers eventually shutting them down. SPIM is a popular target for consumer IM networks such as Yahoo, MSN, AOL, and others.
- **Spoofing or vishing**. Let's say you have set up a locked conference call for your company—for example, a board of directors meeting. You are only letting in known Caller IDs to this conference. You disabled the annoying meeting participant entry chime sound so that late joiners do not disrupt the conference. During this conference you outline your plan and strategy to the board and maybe announce a few new product ideas. Next thing you know, a month down the road, someone else has produced the very product you were designing, to spec. Now how could that happen? Well, spoofing is one way. A spoof is a caller who you did not want joining a conference call who masked his Caller ID with another one. In this scenario, it's a Caller ID from the list of Caller IDs you will accept in your locked conference. Once in, all the spoofer has to do is listen

to your conference call. Spoofing happens often and is more common now in prank calls. All a spoof caller has to do is use a hack to change the Caller ID of his line, in this case a Session Initiation Protocol (SIP) endpoint, and start calling. Expecting a call from your loved one, answer the call, and it's a salesman? Yeah, spoofing is a pain.

n **Denial of Service (DOS) attacks**. DOS attacks are not new; they have been around for as long as I can remember. A DOS attack is simply a process in which an attack on a server or service is so great that it prevents the server from providing service and can be performed with buffer overflows and other means of abundant media and data overflow to the server, either shutting the server down completely or consuming all its resources. DOS in a voice and unified communications world can be detrimental if a company, let's say an enterprise organization, is fully using a voice and UC system as its primary platform. If a DOS attack occurs, it can shut down data transfer, including voice communications data within minutes, preventing a company from receiving or making calls and bringing business to a halt.

# Voice and Unified Communications Security Solutions

Even though the threats discussed in the previous section may be enough to make you not invest in or purchase voice and unified communications products and services, these threats are easy to thwart. By choosing securely architected voice platforms and using industry recognized security products, voice and unified communications products and services can be secured and monitored without a problem.

Let's discuss the following ways to secure your Microsoft Voice and Unified Communications platform:

n **Secure platform architecture**. Microsoft's voice and UC products and services, unlike many of its competitors are based on a secure communications platform leveraging identity security as well as standards-based security protocols such as Transport Layer Security (TLS) and leveraging digital security certificates.

n **Industry-recognized security products**. Today, there are many products to choose from to protect your VoIP system from security threats such as SPIM, vishing/spoofing, DOS, and more through Microsoft and Microsoft partners or even through non-Microsoft partnered solutions. Some of the top VoIP security providers include

n Symantec
n Trend Micro
n Quest Software
n Akonix
n Microsoft

There are even more vendors than those in the preceding list that provide quality voice communication security products, but these are the products I have experience working with. I must say that I am a bit biased in using Microsoft and Symantec software for securing products such as Microsoft Exchange Server and Microsoft Office Communications Server (OCS), but I am equally impressed with products such as the monitoring and anti-SPAM solutions for Exchange and Office Communications Server offered by Quest Software.

## Providing a Secure Platform Architecture

Microsoft, as with all of its products, developed a communications platform from the ground up based on industry standards. This was also carried over in the application of standards-based security architecture to thwart common security risks. Microsoft holds a significant market share in both consumer and enterprise computing, and they are aware that the hacking community views them as a primary target.

Using standards-based security protocols such as TLS and Mutual Transport Layer Security (MTLS) and integrating identity-based security applications such as Microsoft Active Directory provides customers with a state-of-the-art unified and voice-integrated communications platform. The following is an overview of how this architecture is applied.

## TLS 101

TLS is a certificates-based encryption and security solution for applications. Evolved from Secure Sockets Layer (SSL) technology that is still heavily in use today to secure Web sites including e-commerce applications, TLS provides both Web and application-specific security and is the standard security protocol for SIP described earlier in the book. For detailed information related to the creation and updates to the TLS protocol, read the RFC 2246 release via http://www.ietf.org/rfc/rfc2246.txt.

TLS requires a Public Key Infrastructure (PKI), which requires certificate configuration and application on both the client and server environments to ensure that end users of VoIP systems and applications can be trusted. This is important as voice and unified communications applications and devices now span private company infrastructures to global consumer-available. Within a PKI environment, a root enterprise Certificate Authority (CA), which issues certificates for servers and clients, is the core of this model. The CA is the root that each certificate trusts in a chain of secure communication. In most instances, server certificates must be trusted on the client device that is trying to connect to them, whether it is a laptop, desktop, or mobile device. Another property of a certificate is the Extended Key Usage (EKU) type. An EKU is a label or type that is applied to the configuration settings of a certificate that identifies what the certificate is being used for.

The following list outlines all the property types for a TLS digital certificate:

- n  Signed public key
- n  Certificate name
- n  Validity period
- n  URL/location of the certificate revocation system
- n  Digital signature provided by the root Certificate Authority

Now, you might ask, how secure is TLS? SSL has been out since the 1990s, so how has this technology not been hacked as of yet? Well, the answer is pretty simple. Too many tools are needed to really hack a TLS connection. With Microsoft technology, for example, you would have to obtain the trusted root CA certificate, a client certificate trust, and in some cases, Active Directory authentication, plus a login and password. Not that easy, eh? Explained more technically, TLS is secure in that there are many layers to the TLS connection. The diagram in Figure 8.1 depicts the architecture of a TLS enabled environment.

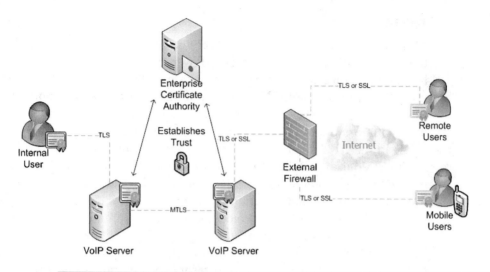

**FIGURE 8.1** Enterprise Certificate Authority

### MTLS

In a multiserver environment, multiple servers must trust each other if they are part of a pool of VoIP or SIP servers. This trust is enabled using MTLS, which is used to configure a trust between VoIP servers. A server certificate is applied to the server (virtual or physical) to enable an MTLS connection from one server to another with an EKU setting of Server Authentication. MTLS is also used to provide secure connectivity to the public Instant Messaging networks, which include Yahoo, MSN, and AOL.

### Microsoft Voice and UC with TLS

Leveraging standards such as SIP and TLS is a great benefit to Microsoft as many other software manufacturers cut corners and create applications based on aging or inflexible technology. I am definitely pleased to say that since I started working with Microsoft in 2001 in the early release of a product called Microsoft Office Live Communications Server 2003 (yeah, they need to work on naming their products), the product team wisely architected their Instant Messaging and Presence-based server product then with SIP and TLS in mind. Today, this architecture continues to form the foundation of Microsoft VoIP security and has been enhanced to include Active Directory authentication as well as fingerprint recognition on VoIP client devices and phones. The following is an overview of how TLS is used within Microsoft's core VoIP products with Microsoft Response Point, which provides VoIP services for small/medium businesses as well as branch offices and with Microsoft Office Communications Server for enterprise customers.

### Microsoft Response Point and TLS

The main goal of the Microsoft Response Point product suite is to provide an easy IP phone system to deploy, manage, and use. As of this writing, Version 1, Service Pack 1 has been released, and we are nearing the Service Pack 2 release of the product. Today, Microsoft Response Point uses TLS to enable secure management and client use of the product through two applications mentioned before with Microsoft Response Point Administrator and Microsoft Response Point Assistant.

Microsoft Response Point Administrator uses TLS to provide a secure connection between the individual running the application on a machine to the Microsoft Response Point Base Unit device. This secure connection is critical because you probably would not want someone making unauthorized changes to your phone system. Again, TLS provides a secure channel of communication as mentioned before so that every time a user runs Response Point Administrator and connects to a respective Response Point Base Unit device, a TLS bridge is created by forcing the user to install the trusted certificate to the user's machine. Once installed, the user is then trusted to connect and enter the password of the Base Unit to make secure configuration changes.

Figure 8.2 provides an overview of how Microsoft Response Point Administrator uses TLS to connect to a Microsoft Response Point (OEM agnostic) Base Unit device.

8. SECURING VOICE

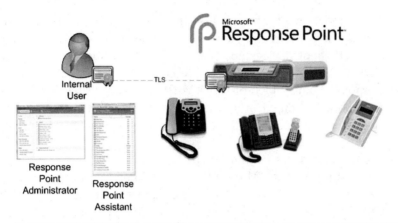

**FIGURE 8.2** Microsoft Response Point and TLS

Microsoft Response Point Assistant works the same way. When a user logs in for the first time, the user is prompted to download a certificate trusted by the Response Point Base Unit. After the certificate is installed, the user then logs in to use the Response Point Assistant application to leverage client features of the system.

Figure 8.3 depicts the prompt provided by Response Point to install the Base Unit trusted certificate from both Response Point Administrator and Response Point Assistant.

**FIGURE 8.3** Microsoft Response Point Administrator Base Unit Certificate prompt

Figure 8.4 depicts the actual Response Point Base Unit certificate.

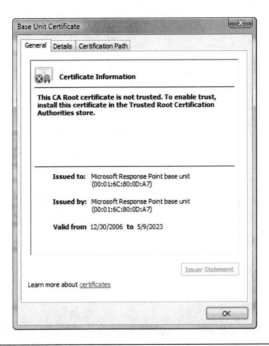

**FIGURE 8.4** Microsoft Response Point Base Unit certificate

Figure 8.5 shows the local computer Certificate Store highlighting the newly installed Response Point Base Unit certificate.

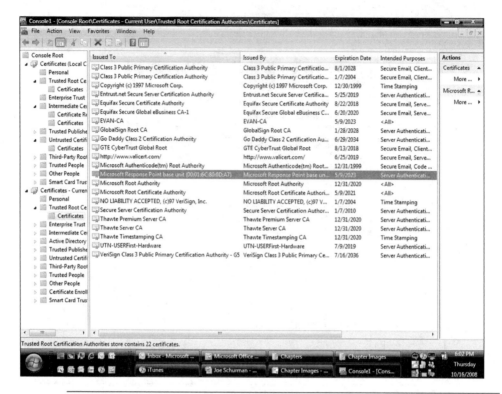

**FIGURE 8.5** Local computer Certificate Store

Providing a secure channel of communication in a small business IP phone system is not only desirable but also is critical in ensuring the security of a growing business. Small- and medium-sized business (SMB) organizations can quickly lose intellectual property and contacts if their communications infrastructure is compromised, and Microsoft's significant investment in SMB as well as enterprise voice and unified communications products and services further differentiates them from their competitors in this space.

### Microsoft Office Communications Server and TLS

Microsoft has been using TLS and MTLS since the release of Microsoft Office Live Communications Server 2003. Leveraging a secure architecture from the ground up and integrating with a secure, identity-integrated security directory, Microsoft Active Directory, provides customers a complete solution for enterprise and midmarket voice communications they can trust.

Microsoft Office Communications Server leverages TLS and MTLS heavily throughout client, device, and sever connectivity enabling a secure channel of communication throughout the network. Microsoft Office Communication Servers use MTLS to securely communicate with each other while clients using Microsoft Office Communications Server client software such as Microsoft Office Communicator Desktop, Web, Phone, and Mobile editions connect securely using TLS. The following is an overview of how TLS and MTLS work within a Microsoft Office Communications Server infrastructure.

Figure 8.6 illustrates how TLS and MTLS are used within Microsoft Office Communications Server architecture.

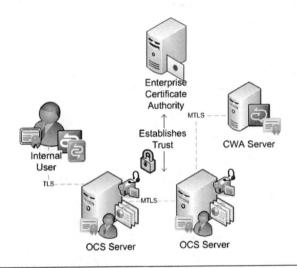

**FIGURE 8.6** Microsoft Unified Communications TLS/MTLS architecture

From a server perspective, OCS servers are configured using an MTLS certificate. This certificate is generated by a CA. Internal OCS servers that exist inside the company's firewall generally use an internal CA such as a Microsoft Windows Server Certificate Authority Service that comes out of the box with Windows Server, Enterprise Edition. This CA generates an internal set of certificates for each OCS server so that they can securely communicate with each other. Externally, OCS Edge Servers and Web Access Servers generally leverage Public Certificate Authorities as most Web sites do to secure their online sites through CAs such as EnTrust and VeriSign, and now even GoDaddy.com offers a cost-effective option for certificate services.

These CAs are used to generate OCS server certificates because remote, mobile, or Web users will be connecting from outside the company's network and will need to trust a certificate service that is publicly known thereby ensuring that each laptop, mobile device, desktop phone, or Softphone will be able to connect. Each mobile device, desktop, or notebook comes preinstalled/prepackaged with a list of trusted root CAs enabling them to recognize and accept these third-party trusted certificates. They are not preinstalled with an internal Windows CA certificate unless these devices are provisioned inside the network using policy enforcement software. So, to ensure that these devices connect without a problem or without having to enforce an internal CA certificate down to the client device or application, OCS enables the use of public CAs to ease the deployment process.

Figure 8.7 depicts the TLS and MTLS certificate trusts internally as well as externally through the OCS Access Edge Server connecting to public CAs to provide secure, remote access to audio/video, voice, conferencing, and Instant Messaging communications.

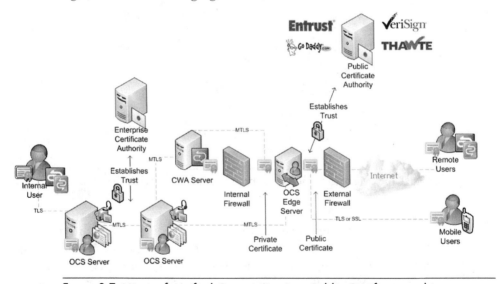

**FIGURE 8.7** Microsoft Unified Communications Public Certificate architecture

By providing TLS and MTLS communication as a standard, out-of-the-box solution, customers have an innovative Unified Communications platform that automatically thwarts DOS attacks or tapping as trying to tap or listen in on a TLS and MTLS enabled connection is nearly impossible. The hacker would have to obtain a certificate, the machine or device the hacker is using would have to be trusted, and the user would have to obtain a Microsoft Active Directory account to sign in to the service.

### Providing a Secure Identity

Microsoft adds to the TLS and MTLS secure architecture by also implementing identity management and authentication services through products such as Microsoft Active Directory, which is required to run OCS, and Microsoft Identity Lifecycle Management (ILM), which is an optional service, but required to connect multiple non-Microsoft directories of users (for example, Lotus Domino, Unix, text-based, and other directory management products).

With Microsoft Active Directory as the core security platform in addition to a standards-based TLS infrastructure, OCS is the most secure Instant Messaging and Voice platform and product suite in the marketplace today. By implementing this identity and authentication service, for a user to hack an OCS environment, she would have to have an Active Directory account plus a TLS certificate to just sign in to the service.

Figure 8.8 is a diagram of the Microsoft Active Directory integration within a Microsoft Office Communications Server infrastructure as depicted using Microsoft Office Communicator to log in.

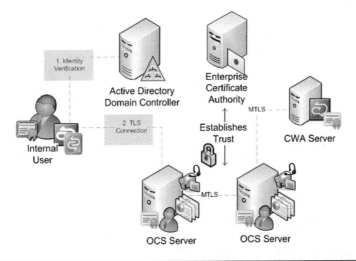

**Figure 8.8** Microsoft Unified Communications Active Directory Authentication

8. Securing Voice

Microsoft also provides policy enforcement through Microsoft Active Directory's Group Policy service. Using the Microsoft Group Policy Object Editor (GPO Editor), IT administrators can further lock down features and services offered by Microsoft Office Communicator from a client perspective and Microsoft Office Communications Server from a server perspective.

Figure 8.9 is a screen shot of the Microsoft Office Communicator GPO template that is used to lock down individual features of the Microsoft Office Communicator client within Windows Server 2008.

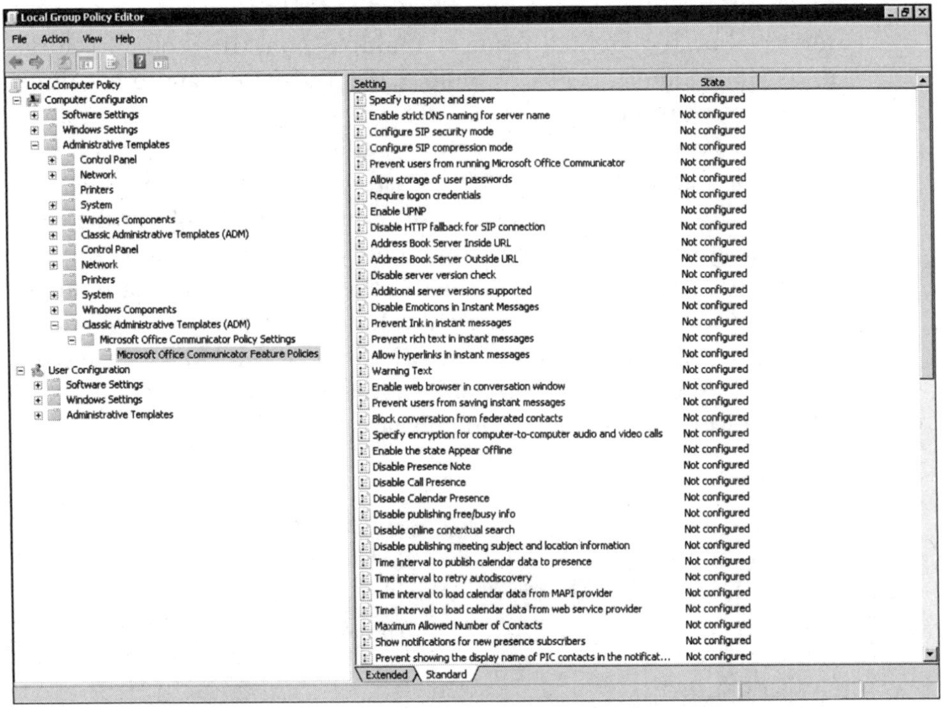

**FIGURE 8.9** Microsoft Active Directory Group Policy object settings/template

By implementing an identity management system through Microsoft Active Directory and locking down vulnerable client features through TLS, MTLS, GPO templates, and leveraging the power of Microsoft Access Edge services for public threats, Microsoft thwarts voice and unified communications potential attacks including DOS attacks, SPIM, and spoofing/vishing easily.

## Instant Messaging Filtering

In addition to TLS and Active Directory integration, Microsoft rounds out its out-of-the-box secure platform by providing the **Intelligent IM Filter,** a free service that provides filtering of unwanted messages, file types, and URLs within Instant Messaging sessions.

To configure the Intelligent IM Filter service, you use the Microsoft Office Communications Server Administrative console—yes, another way to configure all OCS services from within one application. Within the console, use the following steps:

1. Right-click on the Microsoft Office Communications Server node in the tree menu on the left either within the OCS Management Console application or the Computer Management console for the OCS Edge Server role as shown in Figure 8.10.

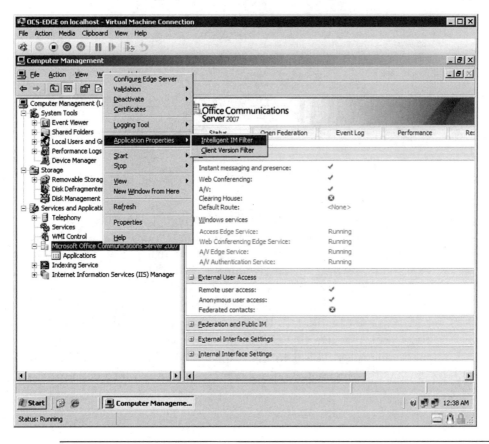

**FIGURE 8.10** Microsoft Office Communications Server Intelligent IM Filter

8. SECURING VOICE

2. Choose the Intelligent IM Filter option as shown in Figure 8.11.
3. In the provided menu, choose how you want to filter instant messages by blocking URLs and/or file types.

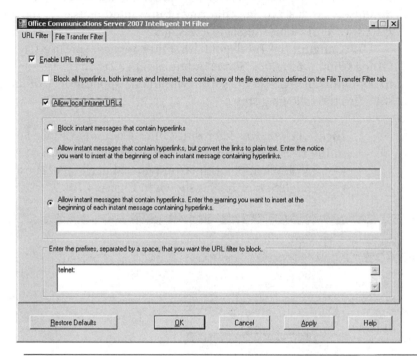

**Figure 8.11** Intelligent IM Filter settings

What's cool about enabling the Intelligent IM Filter service on the OCS Edge Server role is that you can filter a specific message for external messages without affecting messages sent inside the internal network, explaining why the filter service must run on all OCS servers that you want to filter Instant Messages on in or outside your network. If the filter service is not enabled on a specific OCS server, messages sent through the server will not be filtered. If you have two servers with differing filter settings, each message that travels through each server applies that server's messaging rules. This is further explained on the Microsoft TechNet Web site via http://technet.microsoft.com/en-us/library/bb936612.aspx.

## Industry-Recognized Voice Security Products

So far, using TLS, MTLS, and Active Directory integration provides a secure voice and unified communications platform to thwart DOS and spoofing/vishing. Handling SPIM is another matter. Although Microsoft Office Communications Server can thwart SPIM using an out-of-the-box Intelligent IM Filtering service, I always recommend that a SPIM and SPAM filtering tool be applied to external and internal servers for further protection.

Microsoft currently provides a product suite called Forefront that secures not only SPAM for enterprise mail for Microsoft Exchange Server, but also provides SPIM and antivirus protection for OCS, Microsoft Office SharePoint Server (MOSS), and Microsoft Windows client systems. This high-end security product suite can protect and provide monitoring service for your entire voice and unified communications infrastructure ensuring that the money and time you have invested in such an innovative system is protected.

Forefront enables filtering, antivirus, malware protection, and detection of bad traffic that tries to enter your network. Forefront receives automatic updates to security patches and other updates from security consortiums and via Microsoft's security division to prevent new viruses or other problems that could thwart your system. For more information on the Microsoft Forefront product suite, visit http://www.microsoft.com/forefront.

Other popular and industry-recognized voice and unified communications security products include

n **Symantec IM Manager**. This service began through a company IM Logic, who I personally vouched for as a Microsoft MVP through a press release in 2005. After IM Logic was acquired by Symantec, further enhancements were made to IM Logic's IM Manager by providing a full security solution for Microsoft Office Live Communications Server and now Microsoft Office Communications Server with features including

l  Antivirus
l  Anti-SPIM
l  Chinese Walls—Separates internal users from communicating with external users or other divisions of the company. Great solutions for financial traders.

- Intelligent filtering of DOS attacks—In addition to Symantec's security applications for messaging, client endpoints, and devices as well as their popular antivirus software, they provide a complete solution for the Microsoft Unified Communications platform. For more information, visit http://www.symantec.com/business/im-manager.

- **Trend Micro Communications and Collaboration Security**. Trend Micro's solution for the Microsoft Unified Communications platform came out about a year after my endorsement of IM Logic. I received a call from Trend Micro asking me what features I would want in a security software platform for what was then Microsoft Office Live Communications Server 2005, pre-SP1. Soon after, Trend Micro released its IM Security software that provides a great security product to enable anti-SPIM, antivirus and intelligent filtering against DOS attacks, and the company continues to improve these features with each revision. Today, Trend Micro has a complete security platform that not only secures the communication network inclusive of IM, messaging, and portals, but also provides intrusion detection. For more information, visit http://us.trendmicro.com/us/products/enterprise/secure-communications-suite/index.html.

- **Quest Software/Akonix.** Known mostly for reporting, management, and diagnostic software, Quest Software acquired Akonix, which provides a full suite of VoIP and Unified Communications security solutions. What's great about this is that customers can purchase a full migration, diagnostics, reporting, and security package from one vendor enabling a much simpler experience. For more information on Quest Software's Microsoft Unified Communications solutions for diagnostics, migration, reporting, and archiving visit http://www.quest.com/unified-communications. For more information on the Akonix VoIP and Unified Communications security suite of products visit http://www.akonix.com.

- **FaceTime.** Popular since the beginning of the release of enterprise IM products such as IBM Sametime and Microsoft Office Communications Server 2003, FaceTime provides secure Instant Messaging, gateway, and auditing solutions for all enterprise and public/social communications services. For more information, visit http://www.facetime.com/productservices/unifiedsecuritygateway.aspx.

In the end, it's up to you and your pocketbook as to how secure you want your infrastructure to be. While there are new threats unique to voice and unified communications scenarios, established best practices for network security, combined with secure communications relying on TLS and MTLS go a long way toward ensuring voice communications remain secure. It's comforting to know that Microsoft's Voice and Unified Communications products provide a secure platform out of the box unlike its competitors who charge for every small feature. That's not innovation; that's taking care of your customers!

# CHAPTER 9

# HOW TO SELL VOICE AND UNIFIED COMMUNICATIONS

After reading about all the features of the products and services presented in this book you might assume selling voice and unified communications products and services would be easy for a Microsoft partner or Microsoft sales representative. Unfortunately, this is not the case. Largely due to products such as Vonage and Skype, which provide consumer-focused solutions with a lack of security or quality of service, VoIP products and services in general have a horrible reputation, definitely scaring businesses away from purchasing and investing in VoIP technology, which is why I changed the title of this book for one! Another reason for VoIP sales trouble has to do with flat-out confusion. What consumer product manufacturers such as Vonage and Skype have done well is provide a simple overview of what their products provide making customers understand that what you see is what you get. Unfortunately companies such as Cisco and even Microsoft have failed to provide simple sales and marketing materials that give customers an easy understanding of their services and products. Instead, these companies provide complex sales materials, vague descriptions of their products, and no clear path including a product roadmap so that customers can understand where these technologies are going and when to invest. To this effect, it has been difficult for anyone to sell enterprise Unified Communications solutions. Hopefully, this chapter provides you with the materials necessary to not only sell but also differentiate yourself from other service providers in the market.

# Know the Lingo

Over the past seven or eight years, I have spent a great deal of time educating Microsoft internal representatives on the internetworking of Unified Communications and telecommunications terminology. I have also spent a lot of time training companies such as Nortel on Unified Communications applications and terminology. These are two completely separate and distinct groups of individuals, and until the past couple of years, they never interfaced with one another. As we moved into converged communication solutions within the Telco industry, the merging of these two groups has become more common and also more complicated. Cross knowledge transfer is happening more so now than ever, and it is becoming easier to educate both parties in an effort to sell both software-based and hardware-based integrated voice platforms. I guess you really have to understand that companies such as IBM and Microsoft are just now getting into the game and will soon, actually are now, leading the pack in innovative voice solutions as mentioned throughout this book. However, when it comes to partners selling this technology, it takes a bit more of an educated individual who understands the full realm and history of this industry. Chapter 1, "The Communications Renaissance," provides an overview of voice and unified communications terminology, but a plethora of information available online and in print can be helpful as well.

To start, I have to say one of the best books on understanding VoIP terms, history, and a general overview of the technology is *VoIP for Dummies* by Timothy Kelly, published by J. W. Wiley. I have also published many documents, and for those of you who learn better via audio/visual, I have published a Webcast on the Evangelyze Communications Web site at http://www.evangelyze.net as well as on my personal site, http://www.schurman.name, titled the "VoIP Primer." Many additional documents and sites also are available to help you; simply conduct an online search.

Understanding the lingo is key from an industry and technical terms perspective, but also understanding the Microsoft Voice and Unified Communications solution portfolio as well is just as important. To this effect, I wrote this book to combine the two, but you can also find a wealth of information provided by the Microsoft Unified Communications Business Group and Business Marketing Organization online at http://www.microsoft.com/uc as well as a plethora of detailed technical information including Webcasts at http://www.microsoft.com/technet.

One of my favorite sites is run by some buddies of mine, Joey Snow and Adam Bomb from the coolest IT Pro group on the planet, the Microsoft TechNet Edge team. The Edge team has conducted many interviews on various topics related to Unified Communications and other technologies via http://edge.technet.com. I was interviewed by Joey at the Microsoft TechEd 2008 conference in Orlando, Florida, as well in regards to what's new with Unified Communications. My interview can be viewed in a Webcast titled "What's Cool with Unified Communications" available at http://edge.technet.com/Media/Whats-cool-with-Unified-Communications. In this interview I mention how Microsoft provides interoperability with the Apple Mac OS X platform. Viewing entertaining and different Webcasts on topics as they relate to Microsoft Unified Communications will help you speak more intelligently about the platform to customers as well as give you an edge on other competitive partners in keeping up to date on the innovative and edgy stuff that is going on as well.

## Understand the Voice and UC Competitive Landscape

If you remember, the telephony industry dates back to the first telegraph introduced more than a century ago. Since this time we have seen dramatic changes from the telegraph to the Unified Communications devices we know today. Through these years, many companies have come and gone, but some evolved and remained strong, and many new kids on the block have challenged the biggest names in the industry.

Gartner (http://www.gartner.com), a third-party research firm, provides an annual Unified Communications Magic Quadrant. Gartner ranks companies that sell or provide Unified Communications solutions using the following categories:

- n Leaders
- n Challengers
- n Niche players
- n Visionaries

Gartner also ranks these companies by their ability to execute and their completeness of vision.

Figure 9.1 is the most current Gartner Magic Quadrant for Unified Communications.

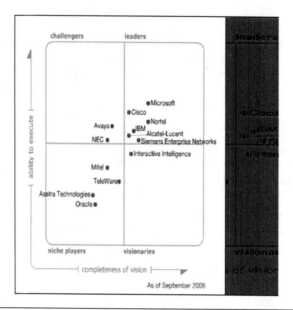

FIGURE 9.1 Gartner Unified Communications Magic Quadrant

Microsoft has been ranked as a leader in this Quadrant for the past two years and has a solid spot in the Unified Communications market as the top provider in the industry based on Gartner's research. In addition to Microsoft, companies such as Cisco, Nortel, IBM, NEC, and Avaya are the top main competitors in this area. Additional players that you would need to be aware of in a competitive sell include Siemens, Shoretel, Mitel, Digium, and Fonality.

In the small-medium business (SMB) space, the same has happened in regards to how telephony systems have evolved, although in a much more recent and faster pattern. In this space, the legacy phone system for a small business, outside a great deal on a used enterprise PBX system, has been the key system or key set devices. Dominant players in this space have included 3COM, Panasonic, Nortel's Norstar line, and Avaya. For the past 20 or so years, these systems have still dominated this space until, in my opinion, Asterisk arrived. Asterisk, now acquired by Digium, provided the first open source PBX system so that developers could configure the phone system features that they wanted and through various gateway devices, were able to connect to any end-user phone device that was SIP compliant. This SIP architecture transformed the SMB telecommunications market, and existing dominant players quickly adapted to the market in response.

Over the past year, dramatic changes, acquisitions, and partnerships have occurred benefiting SMB organizations in that now a more afford-able, extensible set of choices is available. In this new market, unknown players such as Fonality, pbxnsip, TalkSwitch, 3CX, trixbox, and others brought sexy new devices and Softphone applications heavily competing in price and feature set to the existing players. Enter Microsoft, a company that stated in 2007 that it would not develop an IP-PBX system for fear of retaliation of the partners that it currently was working with to extend its current voice platform. Well, they kind of kept their promise until this new small business IP phone system, code named Edinburgh was released. Microsoft designed and developed the phone system software and left the firmware and hardware manufacturing up to a few OEMs as mentioned earlier in the book, creating the first ever Microsoft IP phone system in Microsoft Response Point. Quickly, media and analyst attention turned to the software giant, which with its version 1 release, dramatically trans-formed IP phone systems forever including speech integration and recog-nition into phone handsets and cutting the entry cost for small business customers by less than half of the closest competitor.

By the release time frame of Response Point Service Pack 1, market analysts claimed the Redmond-based giant's small business IP phone sys-tem the most innovative, award-winning system in the market. Now in Service Pack 2 and with an eye on a global market with the introduction of Response Point into EMEA and APAC regions, Response Point has quick-ly taken over as an IP phone system to reckon with.

So how do you separate the marketing hype from reality? Unfortunately this is difficult because you need to be somewhat experi-enced with these competitive products to sell against them. What's really sad is that it seems as if every SIP or PBX system on the market just copies the feature sheet off each other, making it darn near impossible to differ-entiate between the different systems. If you try to highlight key cost com-parisons just by using Web marketed data, same problem.

So, to really competitively sell a Microsoft VoIP solution versus key competitors, you have to contact each manufacturer and pretend you are an actual customer to obtain real price quotes. In the course of two com-petitive projects that I have worked on and commissioned in both the small business and enterprise areas, I have captured a lot of information based on my experience working with each vendor. The following information is an overview of what you need to know about these vendors when trying to sell Microsoft's small business or enterprise VoIP products.

9. HOW TO SELL VOICE AND UNIFIED COMMUNICATIONS

## Microsoft Versus Cisco

Type this subtitle into Google and you will receive a ton of information on this topic, both real and marketing hype. Unfortunately hardly anyone at Microsoft has taken the time to truly understand how Cisco's Unified Communications platform works, so a lot of false information is out there from folks just drinking the Kool-Aid! Several months ago, my firm was commissioned to provide a detailed side-by-side comparison combining Microsoft and Nortel's Unified Communications solution as part of the Microsoft Innovative Communications Alliance versus the newest release from Cisco with Cisco Unified Communications Manager (CUCM) 7.0 release. The purpose of this commission was to dispel the ease of integration that Cisco promised with Microsoft's front-end UC applications to Cisco's back-end presence and PBX systems and phones. This is a pretty big deal because at the time Nortel and Microsoft only provided direct SIP connectivity between vendor solutions, and everyone else has to use a telephony gateway product to integrate.

So, as part of this study, our firm became partners with Cisco—we were already partners with Nortel—and built out our infrastructure at the Evangelyze Communications Datacenter in Houston, Texas, with a set of Cisco Unified Communications software and devices as well as a set of Nortel CS1000 hardware and Unified Communications software, tying both to a Microsoft Office Communications Server (OCS) 2007 and Microsoft Exchange Server 2007 environment for testing and experience. Throughout this process we really only had problems understanding how to implement the new Cisco solution based on lack of experience, not based on lack of product documentation or capability/functionality. And so, at the end of this study, we documented our results in a published whitepaper and presented the research via a hosted/recorded Webcast on our Web site via http://www.evangelyze.net. The bottom line was that these products provided the same end-user experience so there were no differences there. Nortel, Microsoft, and Cisco have sexy and cool add-on hardware devices that look and work great, and provide the same features. Both solutions provided us the ability to simultaneously ring multiple phone numbers or DIDs, allowed us to connect to our SIP Trunking services with Junction Networks just fine, our DIDs worked fine, and so on. The main difference was the learning curve, the extra effort needed to align each application setting perfectly with Cisco's software to ensure proper and quality connectivity to their services and bottom line cost! Cost was the main differentiating factor here. The cost for Cisco's UC solution is nearly double that of a Microsoft Unified Communications solution. With the Nortel add-on, the cost difference was less than half, but still more expensive. We also provided a power/energy draw test as I am known for the cocreation and marketing of the Microsoft Unified Communications Green story. Using energy calculators, we estimated that Cisco's devices drew at least 2 times the amount of energy as Nortel's. This includes routers and phone devices. For an SMB organization like mine, already having to pay a premium for energy use at my datacenter, this is not an option. So outside cost, energy tax, and slight complexity in implementing the solution from an administrative standpoint, both solutions really provided the same feature set from an end-user perspective, but note this is by using a Microsoft/Cisco joint Unified Communications solution.

When looking at Cisco's Unified Communications solution versus Microsoft's Unified Communications platform, there is no comparison. Cisco's system is just too expensive and the Cisco Call Manager (CUCM) 7.0 software is dependent upon Linux. We did find the administrative process to be quite easy though and were pleased with the Cisco CUCM and Cisco Unified Presence Server (CUPS) installation that only took around three hours to complete. However, to enable PSTN support and order the appropriate cards and networking equipment from Cisco to enable these services, complexity doubled and so did the cost.

Hand over fist, Microsoft slaughters Cisco based on the following top three categories from our perspective:

n   **End user intuitiveness**. I am really big on simplifying the user's desktop. Having to open separate applications is a pet peeve of mine, so right off the bat, I hated using Cisco's Personal Communicator application (see Figure 9.2). I like the flexibility of having Microsoft Office Communicator's menu of features available to me within the applications I use on a daily basis, including Word, Excel, PowerPoint, SharePoint, and especially Outlook. Everyone uses Outlook for e-mail. If they don't, they just don't get it. If I use Cisco's Personal Communicator application, this is yet another window to send an Instant Message or participate in a conference call. With Microsoft, it's integrated directly within the Microsoft Office suite.

**Figure 9.2** Cisco Personal Communicator (source: http://www.cisco.com)

I explained the benefits of enabling Unified Communications in a collaborative environment earlier in this book, and this is a big reason why Cisco fails to deliver. Now if Cisco can work in an API or add-in for the Office suite, then I would feel slightly better about its UC solution. The Cisco Personal Communicator application is not unattractive, it's just not integrated. Until then, Cisco needs to hire some better programmers!

n **Administrative ease.** Cisco is many years of development behind Microsoft in this area. From Microsoft's SMB VoIP solutions such as Response Point to Microsoft's Unified Communications stack, they pay attention to IT pros and administrators. Cisco has its own management and reporting tools that do not integrate with any other application such as NetIQ, Quest Software, or any Windows Server apps except for the event viewer, and that is a stretch. What I love about Microsoft's UC servers is that I can manage everything from one Management Console. I can see what is going on with my Exchange Server for e-mail to what's going on with IM and down to the phones and Softphone apps to see what my VoIP Quality of Service is like from one view. Can't do that with Cisco!

n **Flexibility for growth.** Cisco does provide a Linksys Small/Medium Business VoIP solution and also provides a Unified Communications Manager Express solution for medium-sized businesses, and obviously Cisco's premier UC solution for enterprise businesses. This is an area where Microsoft still needs a lot of work, but Microsoft does provide a flexible growth plan for adding OCS and Exchange Servers as needed, and this does not require the exorbitant licensing fees that Cisco requires. Branch office solutions are on their way, and soon Response Point will have some kind of interface for OCS. Between Response Point and Cisco's Linksys solution, there is no comparison; Response Point wins hands down in every category. Bridging the gap from Response Point to OCS Server is going to happen soon, so I'm not worried. In the meantime, it is still much easier to add OCS and Exchange Servers in to accommodate for growth even within multiple geographies.

For more detailed information on my Microsoft versus Cisco discussion, I have a few free online Webcasts and white papers available for viewing at your leisure via http://www.evangelyze.net. For information on the Cisco energy tax, visit http://www.nortel.com, and for the Microsoft and Nortel Unified Communications Green story, visit http://www.evangelyze.net.

## Microsoft Versus IBM

Having worked for both companies, I really do come at this one from a nonbiased perspective. IBM is slowly putting together, with the help of voice partners such as Cisco, a competitive Unified Communications platform that will surprise most everyone as the current attention to the competitive landscape is between Microsoft and Cisco. When I began working with Microsoft in 2001 in the area of enterprise Instant Messaging and collaboration, IBM was our top competitor. Previously when I worked for IBM, leaving in 2001, we had no competitor; Microsoft was the new kid on the block. Around this time, I worked on many competitive analysis projects and also provided a ton of consulting services moving IBM customers, primarily global banking institutions over to Microsoft Office Live Communications Server and Exchange Server from IBM's IM platform, Sametime and IBM's e-mail platform, Domino.

Today, Sametime has been enhanced with IBM's new Lotus collaborative suite that now includes enhanced web conferencing, Instant Messaging, and now voice integration with multi-voice platform vendors. To be honest, I see IBM as more of a threat than Cisco in this space from a platform perspective as I believe the next wave of Unified

Communications and VoIP competition will be the platform play and how companies integrate voice communications into their Line of Business applications to improve their day-to-day activities. IBM is poised for this, not Cisco, and has a deep developer platform and following as well to make this happen and directly compete with Microsoft. Extending voice to web services applications like WebSphere and virtualization products is only just beginning and IBM is ready for this challenge. Not to mention, they have some of the brightest developers and architects in the industry.

Figure 9.3 depicts the new IBM Sametime client application.

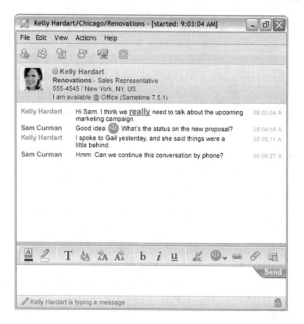

**FIGURE 9.3** IBM Sametime client (source: http://www.ibm.com)

From a competitive perspective, IBM has an equally attractive collaborative suite in IBM Lotus software. Complete with word processing, spreadsheet, presentation, Instant Messaging, Web conferencing, and now voice, with a move into Web services and virtualization, IBM will be Microsoft's top competitor in this space from a software-powered voice perspective. For more information on IBM's Lotus suite for Unified Communications and Collaboration, visit http://www.ibm.com/lotus.

## Microsoft Versus Nortel, Avaya, Siemens, and NEC

Grouping these telecommunications players together in a compete strategy against Microsoft is fine in that each of these companies provides a similar Unified Communications offering. Microsoft, as with Cisco, provides an integrated UC solution with each of these vendors leveraging their Private Branch eXchange (PBX) hardware and phone systems with Microsoft software on the desktop. Separately, each vendor has its own Unified Communications platform, but I would not say it is completely unified. For example, Nortel has a complete voice solution, with voicemail, simultaneous ring, presence (away, available, in a call, for example), follow-me services, and so on, but there is no collaborative solution that truly ties into a desktop office suite whether it's IBM or Microsoft. They depend on the existing customer's solution and force them to use separate applications on the desktop, which are really not user interface friendly compared to IBM's or Microsoft's offering. However, these are voice systems, not collaboration suites, so they perform what they were designed to do, very well. Unfortunately, we are still talking about requiring hardware-based PBX systems, phone devices, and so on, so as Microsoft and IBM tackle the new Virtual PBX with SIP Trunking, these solutions will soon become archaic.

Nortel has separated itself from this a bit in that it is are codesigning virtual PBX systems with Microsoft, but others such as Avaya and NEC are really not making strides in virtualizing their platform like they should. Avaya has a strong play currently as its devices and applications that manage these devices have been around for decades, so customers are comfortable with them. Avaya also has a cool One-X platform that does provide more of a collaborative play with mobile tie-ins and portal integration, but it is a bit of a rigid platform and not as extensive as the Microsoft Unified Communications platform with .NET integration. NEC has been a dominant telecommunications provider alongside or more so than Cisco has been for decades. The Japanese-based giant has a huge customer base, and they are starting to have conversations about providing a more software-driven voice platform, but again, they're a bit behind the curve. However, they have the finances, talent, and experience to make a sudden change in architecture, and I expect them to be a dominant player in the future. NEC's Univerge platform is slick, but again, like Cisco, Avaya, and many others, it's not truly tied into the customer's daily information worker platform. This, again, is where Microsoft has the larger play. Even if you stack up the voice client applications from NEC, Cisco, Avaya, Siemens, and so on, they don't compare to the user interface and integration of the Microsoft Office suite or IBM Lotus platform.

Customers do not need another application, they need integration and solutions. The customer should be able to choose whatever phone device or PBX they want. The future of voice services in regards to application integration and development will provide ubiquitous integration to multi-vendor telecommunication devices and modalities of communications, so when you are talking about comparing platforms between Microsoft and Cisco, Avaya, NEC, Nortel, and others, it is easy to see why Microsoft is a leader as these vendors do not have a platform, they have tools. If these vendors do not start moving towards virtualized platforms or ease the integration of direct SIP connectivity to their devices, we will all look back 20 years from now and realize that these once giants of telecommunications are obsolete.

On another note, Siemens, like Nortel, is developing virtualized PBX systems and new SIP-based phone devices and Softphones that are in line with the vision of the future of Unified Communications. Currently, Siemens has a large play, as do Avaya, Nortel, Cisco, and NEC, in hardware-based voice communication solutions for small/medium businesses as well as enterprise organizations with PBX hardware and phone devices with its HiPath series, but what's more interesting is what Siemens is doing with its OpenScape portfolio of voice products by focusing on software-powered voice solutions rather than hardware.

In regards to how Microsoft compares to all these existing voice and unified communications providers, to me, it really comes down to the future of software plus services. There are only two companies really focused on this strategy right now, Microsoft and IBM. Both companies realize that all this unnecessary, annoying, and expensive telephony hardware will be nonexistent in the next 5 to 10 years and the power of software and hosted services are what will bring innovation to voice communications. IBM and Microsoft, who have had a love/hate relationship in the past, will go head-to-head in this area of hosting voice through data centers and extending some very cool industry and cross-horizontal voice-enabled business applications that will set them apart from Nortel, Mitel, Shoretel, and all the other "tels" out there. It will come down to the software plus services platform strategy. I predict Microsoft will be victorious in this challenge as the open development opportunity for third-party developers and extensibility of the Microsoft platform to multiple Line of Business, multiple browsers, and a plethora of devices will be key as well as the ability to run this new software-powered voice service across a multitude of datacenters worldwide. This will enable companies to outsource their voice communications platforms to online hosted services and is the future and in-line with Microsoft's voice strategy for the next 10 years.

For more information on Siemens Unified Communication solutions, visit http://enterprise.siemens.com/open/us/oucs; for Avaya, visit http://www.avaya.com; for NEC, http://www.necunified.com; and for Nortel, http://www.nortel.com/uc123.

## Microsoft Versus the SMB VoIP Competition

Microsoft Response Point entered into the small business IP phone marketplace about two years after manufacturers such as Fonality, trixbox, TalkSwitch, 3CX, pbxnsip, and a few others showcased their ability to create and provide a software-integrated SIP platform that included Softphone applications, extensibility to multivendor phone devices, and a dramatically lower entry price as compared to vendors such as Nortel, Avaya, Panasonic, and others. In this highly competitive SMB market, Microsoft stunned the competition in many ways, most notably as follows:

- n **Free software**. Stopping most competitors dead in their tracks, Microsoft released version 1 of Microsoft Response Point with an interesting new sales incentive—they gave away their software and provided a system with comparable features to existing IP phone system competitors with no additional licensing fees. Yes, you can say "wow" now! Additionally, Microsoft added a small upgrade—kidding—with direct SIP Trunking integration in the SP1 release as well as Click-to-Call integration, Presence, and custom music integration, again, for free!
- n **Innovation**. If you were sitting around a couple of years ago thinking of a way to truly innovate existing phone devices/handsets, I'm pretty sure that speech recognition was among the top five on your list. For some reason, no other manufacturer had the foresight to do this. Fortunately XD Huang and his brilliant team at Microsoft Research came to market with the first IP phone system handset that included a beautiful blue button that gave users the ability to tell the phone what the user wanted it to do—whether placing a call, retrieving a parked call, and more importantly, transferring a call. I say more importantly, because with all IP phone systems, either in the enterprise or SMB market, transferring a call is flat-out annoying. You have to remember key codes, and for most new phone users, a majority of transferred calls are dropped. With the "Blue Button" transferred call drops have ceased forever. Simple, innovative features like these—again, provided for free—slaughtered Microsoft's SMB competition from the start.

n **Power to the people**. One problem with all phone systems today is that you always have to go through the rarely seen telecom administrator for your company to make any changes to your account, or you have to whip out the key code bible to find out which key codes are the right ones to accomplish such a simple task as forwarding your phone calls over to a colleague or secretary when you're going on vacation. Microsoft decided to nix this problem off the bat by providing end users with an application like Microsoft Response Point Assistant. Through this application, end users have the power to change their dial plans, modify their out of office settings, control their greetings, change call forwarding plans, and even import contacts from Outlook to enable voice dialing on their handsets. Oh, yeah, this is free too!

So what is the rest of the competition doing? Outside of running scared and going out of business, alliances are being made from the open source world with dominant vendors such as Cisco, Avaya, Nortel, and other small players such as Digium. Quickly realizing the business value of open source telephony, Digium snatched up Asterisk to provide a complete solution for SMB and now even enterprise customers to sort of compete with Microsoft. Unfortunately the problem with each of these vendors is that when the vendor finally catches up to Microsoft in features, the cost then outweighs the solution, so Microsoft wins in price. I spent a great deal of time coming up with a competitive analysis study for Microsoft, on my own dime, and created a competitive battlecard, which is included on our resource Web site via http://www.schurman.name/microsoftvoice.asp and referenced in Appendix A, "Closing Comments and Resources." This content is also published on the Microsoft Partner Program Web site for Microsoft Response Point via http://www.microsoft.com/partner; search for "Response Point" to see side-by-side comparisons between Microsoft Response Point and the popular competitive solutions in this market. I also put together a Webcast titled "How to Sell Microsoft Response Point," which is hosted on the Microsoft Partner Program Web site for Response Point as well as on our Evangelyze Communications media site via http://www.evangelyze.net. These two resources will help you competitively sell against these key competitors, but I suggest you research these solutions for yourself as well to gain your own perspective.

Bottom line, plenty of software-based and hardware-based Unified Communications solutions are out there. To me, as a consumer, CEO, and general technologist what it comes down to is integration and ease of use. Whoever provides an open platform for developers to integrate line of business applications, but still enables a truly integrated voice platform leveraging virtual or hardware-based voice communications will win. Those who fail to see the value of integrating voice services into day-to-day applications such as the Microsoft Office suite or IBM Lotus suite will fail, and those who do not design voice services for hosted and virtualized environments, will be out of business.

## Leverage Microsoft Voice Sales Incentive Programs

So, after you build a general knowledge of the competitive landscape by researching each major competitive offering, how do you convince a customer to buy a Microsoft Unified Communications or VoIP product? It's hard to sell a company that has used the same voice vendor for decades on the benefits of tying voice into applications or a particular platform, so Microsoft has created many sales incentive packages for Microsoft partners through Business Investment Funds (BIF) programs for Voice Pilots and Lighthouse Pilots on a global basis. Now, you will have the arsenal content plus some cold hard cash to help incentivize a customer to listen. In addition to this, Microsoft Financing also can assist in funding up to 100% of consulting services needed to architect, integrate, and install a Microsoft Unified Communications and VoIP solution for a customer. On top of this, if the customer or solution fits the requirements, Microsoft will commission a case study and highlight the solution online! Now that's incentive. In addition, Microsoft has specifically assigned voice partner account managers, business development managers, sales solution professionals, and technology sales professionals to help you close the deal within each region and district of the world.

So how do you get started? The following sections outline the steps you must take to quickly engage with Microsoft to start selling Unified Communications and VoIP solutions.

### Step 1—Become a Microsoft Partner

The Microsoft Partner Program community is the most elaborate, informative, and caring partner program of any IT partner program I have ever known, and I've been in this industry for more than 15 years. To become a

Microsoft Partner and join the Microsoft Partner Program, visit http://www.microsoft.com/partner and sign up for free. There are many different levels of this program ranging from a Registered Member to a Gold Certified partner, each providing resources and guidance to help you get started in selling and learning about Microsoft VoIP products as well as many other products and services Microsoft offers. More specifically, there are partner programs for Microsoft Unified Communications and Microsoft Response Point described as follows:

n **Microsoft Voice Specialized Partner (VSP).** To become a VSP—and the rules may change by the time this book is in print—currently you must meet the following requirements:

1. You must have a certified Microsoft Unified Communications platform running for your company internally. This includes Microsoft Exchange Server 2007 with Unified Messaging, Microsoft Office Communications Server 2007, now with R2, VoIP and Telephony integration with some kind of virtual or approved PBX vendor, and end users running Microsoft Office Communicator 2007 R2. After about a $20,000 to $100,000 investment, you're there! (I know what you're thinking—call us at Evangelyze Communications, and we can help square you away with a more affordable solution for this.) Once your infrastructure is completed, you will then need to go through a certification test with a Microsoft assigned representative. Sunita, our Microsoft certification UC rep, was a little surprised when we initially used our completed research project for a completely virtual Unified Communications environment on the 2007, non R2 platform right off the bat. Anyway, we squared up our actual, hardware-based solution, and we were certified in a few weeks. This is a minimal requirement to be in the program so if you can't commit to building out an internal Unified Communication infrastructure, sorry.

2. You must have certified Microsoft Exchange Server and Microsoft Office Communications Server consultants in your company. To become certified, send your consultants to one of Microsoft's training courses including the Microsoft Unified Communications Voice Ignite course and also the Microsoft Unified Communications Sales Ignite course. This training will prepare you and them for their voice certification exams.

3. You must have at least a few consultants or representatives from your company attend the Voice Ignite and Sales Ignite training mentioned in the previous task.

4. You must meet a Unified Communications Microsoft Partner Program Competency. For details on these competencies and updates, visit https://partner.microsoft.com/US/40029082?PS=95000124.

n **Microsoft Response Point Value Added Reseller (VAR).** To join the partner program for Microsoft Response Point, you must be at least a Microsoft Partner Registered Member. After registering, you then need to become a Value Added Reseller for at least one Response Point OEM vendor, currently Aastra, D-Link, and Quanta. Each partner program is free to join so don't worry! After doing so, you are then connected to the Microsoft Response Point team, who, if you are educated on the product enough, will list your company as a partner on its Web site so that customers can contact you to purchase Response Point products. In each sales engagement, you will make around a 10% margin on hardware sales as well as any services revenue for installing and managing the customer's Response Point system.

## Step 2—Engage with Microsoft

After becoming a Response Point or UC partner, your next step is to start rubbing shoulders with the right folks at Microsoft. Each group has its own set of specific resources to help you sell and market your services described as follows:

n **Get to know your Unified Communications Voice Partner Account Manager (PAM).** After becoming a Microsoft Certified Voice Specialized Partner, you are assigned a Voice PAM in the region where you are headquartered. Each one of these Voice PAMs is excellent and easy to work with and will guide you in regards to how to work together with Microsoft on Microsoft-funded or non-funded customer sales and technical engagements.

n **Meet the Response Point marketing and business development team**. The marketing team is currently headed up by Richard Sprague, a seasoned veteran from Microsoft who has extensively built up the marketing and product readiness planning for Microsoft Response Point in partnership with the business development team headed by John Wang and Rex Backman. Each of these resources applies a personal approach to Response Point partners, especially early on because the number one focus of the product in its early stages is to build awareness. Anyone willing to help with this process is treated very well! Complete with a VAR council, constant updates, and program packages for Response Point partners, this team has done its job well and continues to do so. Another interesting resource of the team is the Response Point blog, http://blogs.technet.com/rp/, which is updated by the Response Point team on almost a daily basis and provides a wealth of updated information.

## Step 3—Differentiate Yourself

I have been working with Microsoft internally on voice and unified communications solutions since the beginning and am currently working with Microsoft Research on what's to come, so I have a bit of an edge on this. Bottom line: Make sure that you separate yourself from the crowd. By 2010, many VSP partners will be able to install the infrastructure side of the UC platform. They will be a dime a dozen. It actually bothers me still that some Microsoft Solution Sales Professional (SSP) and Technical Sales Professional (TSP) reps still focus only on the infrastructure side of this and not the integration and development, but I guess they have to be narrow-minded and shortsighted because that's what they are paid to do. However, they will soon be wondering—after the software is installed—how they are going to make additional money and make their quotas. The answer is with line of business integration and VoIP/UC development solutions. So for those of you who do this today, and you know who you are, take the blinders off and get ready.

Luckily, Evangelyze Communications does this already. We can install and support every voice integrated infrastructure platform out there and can do it quickly. We have templates such as design documents, customer presentations, installation guides and shortcuts, as well as predeveloped virtual server environments for Proof of Concept environments at the ready to speed the deployment life cycle of an engagement. We call this methodology and kit of UC solutions the EC UC 1-2-3 package. This package or methodology differentiates us from other vendors. However, we don't focus on this piece of the puzzle as this work has been done a hundred times or more by my team of primarily former Microsoft employees who are gurus on the Microsoft UC platform. Instead, we lead with customized Unified Communication solutions that customers can actually use to enhance the way they communicate.

What's awesome about this is that we further differentiate our firm from small and even global system integrators and vendors in the VSP program but also help Microsoft compete against other vendors such as Cisco, Avaya, and Siemens, but especially IBM, because, and I'll say it a million times, it's not the features of a Unified Communications platform that truly transform a business, it's how it affects an end user's daily life—their productivity—that makes a difference. So we have designed solutions such as an intelligent chat solution called SmartChat as highlighted in Chapter 7, "Customizing Voice Applications," as well as Web scheduling for Office Communications Server conferences and on-premise voice and video meetings. We've also connected small business IP phone systems such as Microsoft Response Point with the enterprise Microsoft Unified Communications platform to provide branch office access without having to pay for long distance fees between offices. These things further separate us from the rest of the VSP pack. The hard part is turning on the lightbulb. It takes time, but it will happen. That's the downside to being way ahead of the curve, but I like it! We pride ourselves on being research freaks! So, again, the focus post-VSP certification should be to differentiate yourself from other VSPs and offer something unique to your end customers making it easier to engage with Microsoft and the customer and especially easy to compete in such a deep Unified Communications market.

Following these steps will help you on-ramp a new Unified Communications services practice or start a new voice and unified communications company for the entrepreneurs reading this book. For more information on this program visit either http://www.microsoft.com/uc or the Microsoft Partner Program via https://partner.microsoft.com/US/40029082?PS=95000124.

**9. HOW TO SELL VOICE AND UNIFIED COMMUNICATIONS**

# Learn How to Sell Voice and UC Consulting Services

Consulting services and application development are where the money is made in selling Microsoft Unified Communications and Microsoft Response Point. To win customer engagements with or without the aid of Microsoft in the sales process, you need to develop your own methodology that shows the customer that you will easily deploy the solution and clearly deliver this engagement on time. Using the following guidance, you learn how to easily engage with an enterprise or SMB customer by leveraging a voice and unified communications sales engagement methodology I created called UC 1-2-3.

## Introducing the UC 1-2-3 Methodology

As mentioned previously, many partners will be selling infrastructure services around the deployment of Microsoft Unified Communications software and required server and telecommunications infrastructure. As a partner, you must differentiate yourself from other partners in this area. I have worked for companies including Compaq, HP, IBM, Microsoft Consulting Services, and Accenture. As a manager in the Microsoft Solutions Organization of Accenture, most of my time was dedicated to building out a new services methodology for specific Microsoft products. Accenture had an edge over many services partners in that they provided clear-cut methodical approaches in how to apply services. Starting from a presales engagement with a customer to a postsales customer review, Accenture cared for its customers throughout the full life cycle of a project.

Many other systems integrators provide the same level of care, but as with many other things in life, the "devil is in the details." To provide professional services to customers efficiently, you have to clearly outline what the engagement will encompass, set expectations up front, but more importantly, ensure that your customer is ready. Many times, we just sell and don't look at the details of a customer's environment, understand their business processes, or interview their business decision makers in how they operate on a daily basis before a project begins. When implementing a solution such as Microsoft Unified Communications, it's important to take everything a company does under consideration. That's why we provide a certain level of due diligence before we even embark on a customer engagement.

Our UC Due Diligence process is a key part of what I call the Unified Communications 1-2-3 program. I designed this program for Nortel Networks when they signed the Microsoft/Nortel Innovative Communications Alliance in 2005. As part of this relationship I was requested by Nortel to meet with all of their services executives and principals to outline and create a new methodology to aid in Nortel's ability to provide Microsoft software and Nortel hardware integrated Unified Communications solutions. Such a methodology had not existed, and I had created something similar before. So my task was to educate the telecommunications giant as they were on point for Microsoft to provide the first series of Unified Communications engagements to select customers to build out case studies to increase awareness of the newly created Microsoft platform to their existing customer base, which was a daunting task in and of itself.

The following plan is what I outlined to Nortel in Raleigh, North Carolina, at the Nortel ICA Collaboration Center and birthed the release of the Evangelyze Communications UC 1-2-3 Services Methodology.

## UC 1-2-3 Business Plan

The purpose in creating the UC 1-2-3 services methodology was to not only shorten the sales life cycle with a customer, but also improve the quality of a Unified Communications deployment. Too many times Microsoft and its partners were too anxious to sell Unified Communications solutions in an effort to build awareness and quickly build case studies in an effort to obtain additional sales activity. This caused problems such as mixed feedback about the Unified Communications solution by customers as well as failed deployment projects that resulted in Microsoft or the partner fitting the bill of infrastructure oversights and scope creep issues. All these problems, though hushed, caused a lot of confusion, arguing, and nights of endless work to rectify.

The problem was simple. Sales reps were overcommitting on features or integration functionality with a customer's existing systems as well as a massive oversight of the customer's internal infrastructure. These problems included not understanding the customer's dial plan configuration, security baselines for operating systems of users who would install Microsoft's client software, additional server and client-based security problems, and many issues with Microsoft's Access Proxy and Edge Server architecture due to the customer's already stringent DMZ and extranet policies.

Another large problem that could not be fixed by technology was the realization of how many representatives of an organization had to be involved in a Microsoft Unified Communications engagement. Because this platform affects the desktop, server, telephony hardware, Internet and intranet, security policy, mobile devices, and directory management, many enterprise organizations quickly found out that this was not a small task. This issue could have quickly resolved by identifying these personnel requirements in the initial planning of the engagement.

I actually dedicated an entire chapter to this problem in my first book, *Microsoft Office Live Communications Server 2005*, published by Wrox Books in 2006, and then further wrote a published internal whitepaper on this problem the same year. Unfortunately most consultants and sales reps in this space have no time to read, so this guidance was missed. Hopefully, given the support I have for this book, this guidance will be applied. I can say that the sales process has improved, and Microsoft has made many efforts to train its sales teams and partners efficiently through programs such as Voice Ignite and Sales Ignite. Our firm has done the same with our internal employees and sales reps as well as for Microsoft on a global scale. But, to make this easy, the UC 1-2-3 business plan clearly identifies key processes to engage during the sales and deployment process as identified in Figure 9.4.

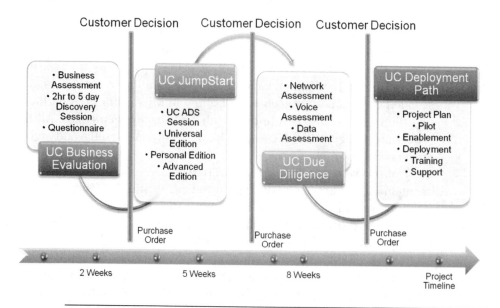

**FIGURE 9.4** UC 1-2-3 methodology

### UC Business Evaluation

As depicted in this model, I focus a great deal of effort on the initial engagement with a customer, truly understanding how the customer would leverage a Unified Communications solution as well as clearly assessing the environment before we step foot inside a customer's network. I call this process the **UC Business Evaluation**. During this process, the customer goes through a survey or questionnaire for the partner to understand how the customer uses telephony and collaboration products today, and it also helps the customer understand what areas Microsoft's Unified Communications platform will provide productivity gains—whether soft or hard Return on Investment (ROI) benefits. The better job that a partner does in this step of the process, the better the customer and the partner will benefit in the end, even if it means that the customer is not ready for this solution or that the partner realizes that Microsoft's solution is not a perfect fit for the customer.

The end result is a deliverable document given to the customer that depicts what was found in this evaluation using a template for each customer that is processed during this step. This deliverable can be charged for just as the carpet cleaners who visit your home charge an estimate fee for a simple cleaning. This is another area where Unified Communications engagements cause problems: Since the solution was released a lot of investment funds from Microsoft and time on the partner's side have gone unpaid, causing a loss of business and time. Through the UC 1-2-3 model, the partner is compensated for their time despite the customer's commitment to move forward. If the customer refuses to pay or the partner is too shy to identify this requirement, the partner can leverage Microsoft's Business Investment Funds to cover some of this time. No matter how cool the solution is, time away from your business or free time should always be compensated.

### UC JumpStart Kits

I first developed a JumpStart kit for Microsoft's Live Communications Server 2005, and then updated the kit for the Service Pack 1 release. Since then, the JumpStart kits have been updated to provide a quick customer on-ramp process for Office Communications Server 2007 R2 and Exchange Server 2007 with Unified Messaging. The purpose of these kits is to help partners easily showcase to a customer how a working Unified Communications environment would look inside a customer's internal infrastructure. Complete with prepackaged and preconfigured Microsoft Virtual Server and Virtual PC environments, the UC JumpStart kits are as easy as turning on a light switch. I created three separate versions of these kits depending on the level of complexity of the customer's infrastructure requirements or sales commitment ranging from a fully packaged edition to a fully integrated edition as explained in Figure 9.5.

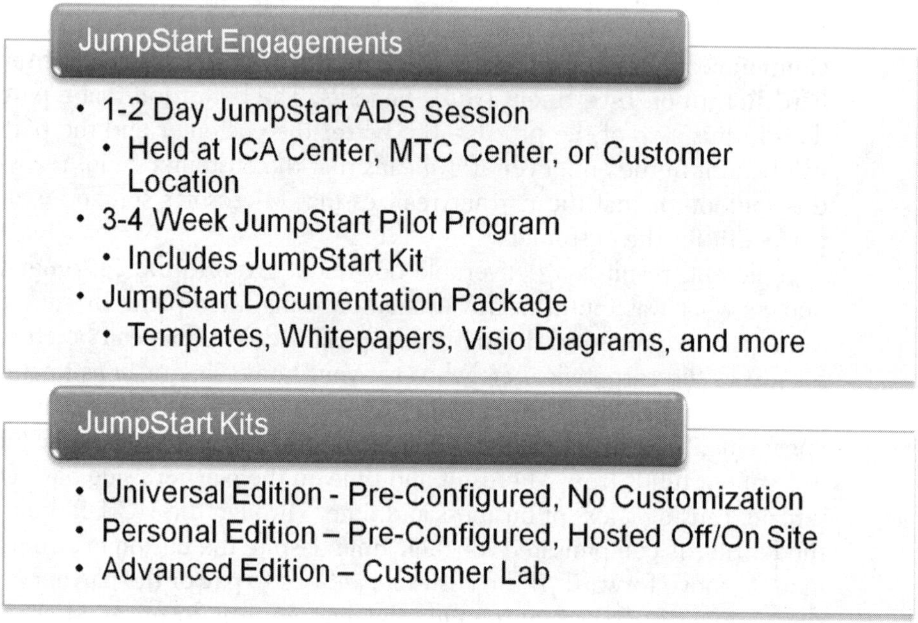

## JumpStart Engagements

- 1-2 Day JumpStart ADS Session
  - Held at ICA Center, MTC Center, or Customer Location
- 3-4 Week JumpStart Pilot Program
  - Includes JumpStart Kit
- JumpStart Documentation Package
  - Templates, Whitepapers, Visio Diagrams, and more

## JumpStart Kits

- Universal Edition - Pre-Configured, No Customization
- Personal Edition – Pre-Configured, Hosted Off/On Site
- Advanced Edition – Customer Lab

**FIGURE 9.5** UC 1-2-3 JumpStart kits

The most basic edition is the Universal Edition kit, which is simply a copy of a Unified Communications fully configured environment available for rent or Virtual Server purchase from the customer. The second level, Personal Edition, is a combination of preconfigured virtual images connected to a customer's internal infrastructure, including a sample of the customer's existing PBX system, VoIP/SIP Trunk, and a preloaded directory of identified users for the customer's pilot engagement for this test. The third level, the Advanced Edition JumpStart kit, is more or less a preproduction engagement with the customer for a defined period of time where the partner fully engages onsite at the customer's location integrating the

Microsoft Unified Communications platform of products with the customer's existing internal applications, phone systems, and other internal infrastructure. This is in contrast to the Universal and Personal Editions, which can be hosted by the partner or Microsoft during the pilot process with the customer.

Bottom line: These JumpStart kits enable a defined period of time in working with a customer during a deployment pilot engagement so as to not waste time getting stuck in day-to-day issues with the customer or running into technical blockers that could prevent the pilot engagement from working, which has caused many delayed or canceled UC product deployments. By enabling a quick start process in this discovery period with the customer, the customer can quickly see the features of the system working in a preproduction environment and can immediately see the value of the solution. This can even aid in additional sales for the partner by letting the customer see how the Unified Communications platform integrates with other applications and devices during the pilot.

Deliverables from this process in the model include an updated architecture guide, which is given during the Architecture Design Session (ADS), which is a Microsoft sponsored meeting where Microsoft, the partner, and the customer outline what products and what level of integration are required for the Unified Communications deployment, a post customer pilot survey where the partner identifies the customer's experience during the pilot, and an updated Statement of Work and proposal for the customer to engage in a full deployment engagement. Again, fees are charged to the customer during this process for the consulting services applied to configuring the environment based on the level of the JumpStart edition, ensuring that even if the customer does not deploy a production environment, the partner has not wasted their time. It's also, again, important to note that in some cases Microsoft can help fund this portion of the project as well, which is why it's important to know your Voice Specialized Partner Account Manager.

### UC Due Diligence

This is the most important part of the UC 1-2-3 model and is the primary reason why some Unified Communications deployments fail. This has to do with performing a proper network, data, and voice assessment of the customer's existing environment. You might wonder why this process is not run up front in addition to the Business Evaluation. The reason is because these assessments take around two weeks to completely analyze the customer's infrastructure and network to determine the technical requirements and dependencies for the Unified Communications deployment. This is also a postcustomer decision to move forward after experiencing the pilot engagement during the JumpStart process. By the end of this assessment phase, the partner will have performed required tests on the network and internally on application dependencies such as security baseline checks for end user client computers and so on. The deliverable of this phase includes an assessment portfolio report to the customer covering each area. This is most definitely a paid engagement. This information is important to the customer and can be used for additional projects or product assessments that the customer embarks on outside the UC engagement.

In order to properly assess a customer's environment during this phase, certain applications are used to capture the data needed for each assessment. One of the most popular tools for monitoring a network and capturing packets and threads of communication throughout an internal network environment is Wireshark. A processor-intensive tool, but effective if used wisely, Wireshark can assess specific protocols and network ports and then output reports based on the captured data for inclusion in the network assessment report deliverable.

Figure 9.6 is a screenshot of a Wireshark capture.

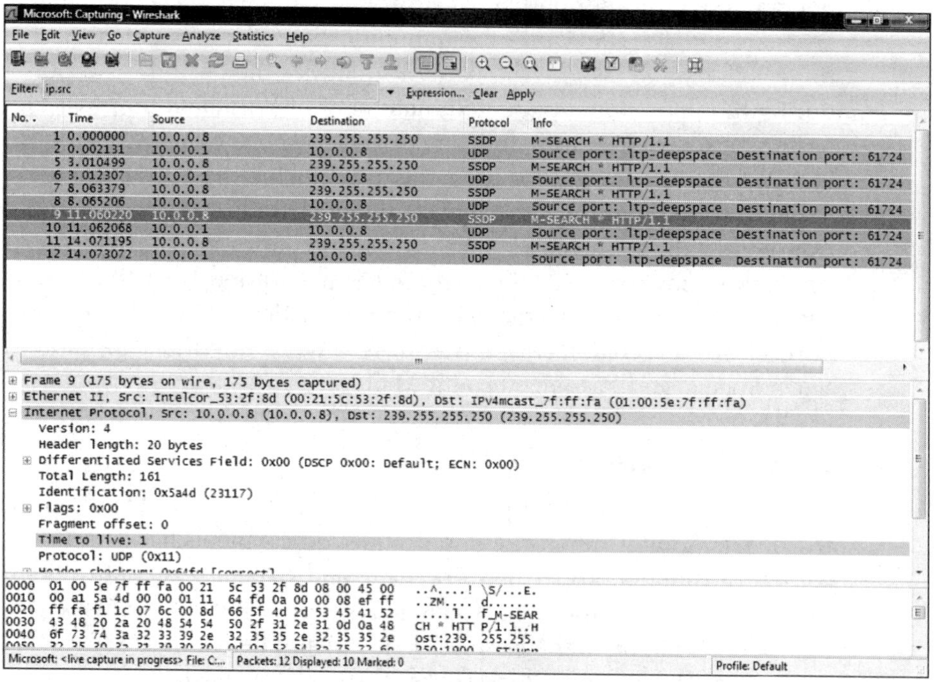

**FIGURE 9.6** Wireshark communications monitoring

To find out more about Wireshark and to acquire this free product, visit http://www.wireshark.org.

Another great tool to use for assessing what server and desktop applications an organization is using is Microsoft's System Center Configuration Manager 2007. This tool can intelligently assess what applications are running inside the organization's network, determine what version of the applications are being used, and can report based on basic or specific criteria you are searching for. For more information on Microsoft Systems Center Configuration Manager visit http://www.microsoft.com/systemcenter/configurationmanager/en/us/asset-intelligence.aspx.

### UC Deployment Path

The last and final phase of the UC 1-2-3 model is the actual deployment. Ironically, this is where most partners that sell Unified Communications services begin! By the time this phase is reached, the partner will have anything and everything they need to know about deploying Microsoft's Unified Communications platform for any customer. The rest of this process is simple and includes a package of document templates including the following:

- **UC Deployment Guide**. This deployment guide outlines the complete process of the project deployment.
- **UC Architecture Guide**. This document outlines the proposed and customer agreed architecture guide including features and functionality required by the customer as part of the project.
- **UC Project Plan**. Amended from the UC Business Evaluation process, the UC project plan is a Microsoft Office Project document that outlines the tasks, hours, timeline, and responsible parties on point for each task. This document can also be uploaded to Microsoft Project Server or Microsoft Office SharePoint Server to ensure the most up-to-date project plan and account for variables such as vacation, waiting periods for equipment purchases, software licenses, and so on.
- **UC Test Plan**. The test plan, the lengthiest document in the package, is a detailed, step-by-step test plan that the responsible party will update per test case identified in the document. These tests range from ensuring proper end user client connectivity from mobile, Web, and PC applications, to phone device connectivity, to server integration and management. Once completed, the partner will obtain customer approval and sign-off on this document as well.

n **UC Blueprint**. This document is provided by the partner to the customer at the end of the deployment and states the entire configuration of the Unified Communications deployment. Through this document, the customer will be able to see details such as the IP addresses, server names, architecture diagrams, software versions, and other pertinent information as a historical document of the project. This is a great document because if a project team's personnel or management changes during the course of the project or years later when new management or IT administration changes occur, the document can be referenced for important updates or understanding of what was deployed.

By assessing the customer efficiently, communicating throughout the entire process, and ensuring that time from all parties involved is compensated, the UC 1-2-3 enables perfection throughout the sales and services life cycle of an engagement and ensures that Microsoft, partners, and customers know exactly what needs to be done, what the deliverables are, and who is responsible. In a nutshell, UC 1-2-3 is as easy as A-B-C.

## Microsoft Response Point 1-2-3

Building on the UC 1-2-3 plan, Microsoft Response Point deployments also needs a proper model for partners to follow to ensure the success of each customer engagement. Though a Microsoft Response Point customer engagement life cycle is dramatically shorter due to the ease of deployment and because Response Point is a self-contained, nonintegrated IP phone solution at this point, it's still important from a services perspective, to ensure quality of a deployment, especially since the product is still new.

To this effect, a UC 1-2-3 lite version has been created to ensure this level of service quality. The RP 1-2-3 services package includes

n **Response Point Assessment**. This assessment document is a lighter version of the assessment document deliverable that is part of the UC 1-2-3 Due Diligence process. This assessment can utilize tools such as Wireshark and others to obtain network and voice bandwidth from the customer's environment to determine whether the customer will be able to provide enough network speed to ensure proper call quality and connectivity within the customer's environment. A great online tool that you can run on-premise/on-site at a customer's location is from CBeyond via http://needforspeed.cbeyond.net. This online analysis tool can assess a customer's network and SIP bandwidth for free, online!

n **Response Point Project Plan**. Similar to the UC 1-2-3 Microsoft Office project document, this project plan document outlines the steps necessary to install, configure, and test a Microsoft Response Point environment.

n **Response Point Customer Artifact**. This document, similar to the UC Blueprint document, outlines the Response Point devices, IP addresses, and architecture that was used to deploy Response Point within the customer's office environment.

Again, the goal of these models is to ensure quality, enforce the proper deployment processes, and get rid of the existing failures that occur in deploying these innovative Microsoft VoIP solutions.

## Sales Summary

In short, every individual and every partner has his own way of selling. Other authors have made a fortune writing sales books and guides, and selling their methodology and documents for profit. I took the other approach. I honestly don't have the time to manage any purchases or IP licensing that I could sell for this information. I thought it would be better for the partner community, better for Microsoft, and most importantly, better for the customer to benefit in leveraging innovative voice technology from Microsoft and building better awareness of these solutions in the marketplace and increasing customer adoption. I hope you, the reader, feel the same!

**9. HOW TO SELL VOICE AND UNIFIED COMMUNICATIONS**

# CHAPTER 10

# THE VIRTUALIZATION OF VOICE

The future of voice and unified communications is in virtualization and more importantly, hosted services. With the ability to create virtual PBX systems run on software platforms like Microsoft's Unified Communications platform and extending voice services and client features through virtual and hosted environments, people, processes, devices, and applications will be connected more than ever. This was the vision of Bill Gates with the .NET initiative almost a decade ago and will soon be realized, in my mind, by the year 2015.

We are already starting to see organizations transform their businesses and adapt to market and customer challenges and changes quickly by leveraging virtual server technology. Now, with the release of Microsoft's Windows Server 2008 Hyper-V, companies can leverage both virtualized hardware and software solutions to on-ramp new applications and services quickly and at a low entry cost as well as a massive reduction in Total Cost of Ownership (TCO).

The purpose of this chapter is to show you what is possible—not necessarily supported but possible—with Unified Communications and VoIP technology from Microsoft leveraging technologies such as Windows Server 2008 Hyper-V and Microsoft Virtual PC.

## Virtualizing Microsoft Unified Communications

In March 2008, I managed a research project through my company, Evangelyze Communications, to test how the Microsoft Unified Communications platform would hold up running the entire platform of servers on virtual environments with Microsoft Windows Server 2008 Hyper-V.

Through this case study, we enabled each of the following components using Hyper-V images using the following configuration:

- SonicWall firewall (external)
- Dell PowerEdge 1450 (DMZ)
  - Microsoft Windows Server 2008 with Hyper-V RC0 64-bit
  - Microsoft Office Communications Server 2007 Mediation Server 32-bit Hyper-V
- Dell PowerEdge 2950 (DMZ)
  - Microsoft Windows Server 2008 with Hyper-V RC0 64-bit
  - Microsoft Exchange Server 2007 with Unified Messaging 64-bit Hyper-V
  - Microsoft Office Communications Server 2007 Edge Server 32-bit Hyper-V
- Dell PowerEdge 1450 (internal)
  - Microsoft Windows Server 2008 with Hyper-V RC0 64-bit
  - Active Directory Domain Controller
  - Microsoft Office Communications Server 2007 Enterprise Edition Server 32-bit Hyper-V
- PBXnSIP hosted PBX service
- Junction Networks Direct SIP Trunk for Microsoft Office Communications Server 2007
  - Seven Direct Inward Dialing (DID) numbers.
  - Configured within Microsoft Office Communications Server 2007 Mediation Server
- Five test users
  - Four Microsoft Windows Vista Service Pack 1 with Microsoft Office Communicator 2007 users
  - One Apple Mac OS X with Mac Messenger 7.1 for Microsoft Office Communications Server 2007 users

The total configuration cost added up to about $15,000 including the Dell hardware, rack storage space in our data center in Houston, Texas, and time spent configuring the service. For a medium-sized organization to a department of an enterprise organization, this service would power around 15,000 to 20,000 users enabled with voice, video, Instant Messaging, and Live Meeting conferencing capabilities. The solution was relatively inexpensive and easy to configure. Although the Microsoft Office Communications Server 2007 solution is not supported until the Office Communications Server 2007 R2 release, the solution worked great, and we had absolutely no issues with voice quality or loss of service. Microsoft Exchange Server 2007 with Service Pack 1 was built to run on Windows Server 2008 Hyper-V, so we did not expect any problems with this service. We were also happy to experience Exchange Server 2007 on a 64-bit platform, whereas Office Communications Server only supported a 32-bit platform so we had to create separate Windows Server 2003 Hyper-V servers as OCS 2007 also did not support Windows Server 2008. This experience was a little frustrating because switching between Windows Server 2008 virtual server images and Windows Server 2003 virtual server images only showcased how archaic the previous server operating system looked and felt in regards to features and functionality. Now with Office Communications Server 2007 R2, all these services are supported on the Windows Server 2008 operating system including Hyper-V.

Enabling all these services within virtual environments provided immediate benefits that we could see major enterprise and especially small- to medium-sized organizations leveraging, including

n **Ease of deployment.** The ability to create Windows Server 2008 Hyper-V virtual server templates for Windows Server 2008 and Windows Server 2003 servers was great in that we could reuse the same base configuration for installing additional Exchange and OCS server roles. Figure 10.1 depicts multiple Unified Communication servers running in a Windows Server Hyper-V state.

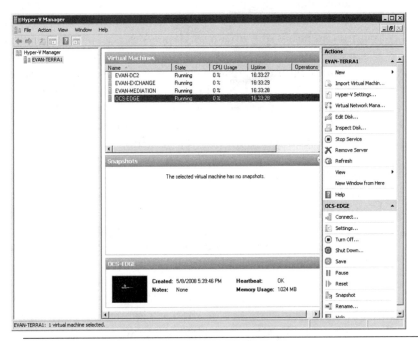

**FIGURE 10.1** Windows Server 2008 Hyper-V Manager

n **Enhanced server backup and migration.** One of the biggest benefits to virtualizing server roles, especially in a VoIP and UC capacity is the ability to migrate virtual images off one server to another if better scalability or performance is needed on a particular server. Another benefit is being able to create shadow backup copies of each Hyper-V server in the case of a potential hardware or software failure.

n **Lower TCO.** Leveraging a Hyper-V environment enables SMB organizations to finally afford a Microsoft Unified Communications solution. Whereas in the past, every OCS and Exchange server role had to be separately installed on different physical hardware, with Hyper-V, organizations can run multiple server roles on one piece of physical hardware. Bear in mind, this piece of physical hardware needs to be designed to support virtualization, which requires a lot of physical memory and processing power, but still the server that we purchased for the bulk of our Hyper-V images totaled $7,500. That is inexpensive compared to running each server role on five different physical servers at a cost of at least $2,500 per server.

n **Better upgrade strategy.** In addition to backups and migration, being able to adapt to future upgrades of the software platform is much easier to manage in a virtual environment. An IT administrator can easily spin up a new Hyper-V server with the latest software and then replace an existing Hyper-V server quickly. Or, an IT administrator can create a copy of an existing Hyper-V server, move the server to a test environment and upgrade the existing software on that server, test how the server functions, and then migrate the server to replace the existing Hyper-V server in the production environment further reducing time and TCO.

After this Hyper-V test, we published our results and additional deployment details on our Web site, http://www.evangelyze.net, so that other organizations and consultants could benefit from these results. The project was a lot of fun, was a great learning experience, and ignited our entire company's interest in Microsoft's Windows Server 2008 and Hyper-V strategy for the future.

By the year 2015, you almost certainly will start seeing virtualized PBX systems leveraging virtual server technology across the marketplace, and this will be the new frontier of Unified Communications competition in the enterprise and SMB markets moving forward.

For more information on Microsoft Windows Server 2008, visit http://www.microsoft.com/windowsserver2008.

## Virtualizing Microsoft Response Point

The Microsoft Research Communications Innovation Center marketing and product team may actually kill me for writing this, but I could not refuse as I am covering the virtualization of VoIP in this chapter. Microsoft Response Point does not have to run on OEM hardware. Yes, you read that correctly. The power of the Response Point system, the Response Point Base Unit software, runs on a CF Flash Card that is physically installed on each OEM Base Unit hardware device. On the CF Flash Card is a pre-configured and loaded Microsoft Windows XP Embedded image running the Microsoft Response Point Base Unit software that powers all the phone system PBX features of the Response Point system on a virtual image.

So, if you want to run and test Response Point in a *completely unsupported manner*, all you have to do is as follows:

1. Create a Microsoft Virtual PC image running Windows XP.
2. Unscrew the top of the OEM Base Unit device and carefully remove the CF Flash Card from the device as depicted in Figure 10.2.

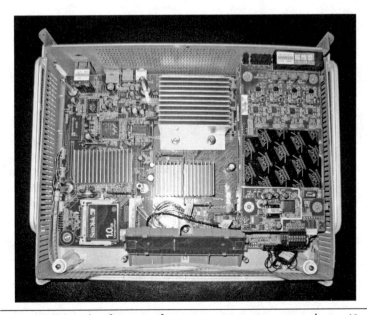

**FIGURE 10.2** Inside of Microsoft Response Point Base Unit device (Syspine Unit)

3. Copy the BaseUnitPrerequisites.exe file and the setup.exe file under the Base Unit folder of the CF Flash Card to a folder on your desktop using a CF Flash Card Reader as shown in Figure 10.3.

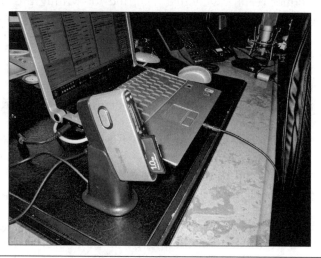

**FIGURE 10.3** CF Card Reader (with Response Point CF Card)

4. The three main requirements for running the Response Point Base Unit software include

  n Base Unit Prerequisites
  n Base Unit setup.exe file
  n Windows XP

5. Once installed, you can run/activate the Base Unit software by choosing the Start menu from the Windows XP Virtual PC image, selecting the Run command, typing **Net start cdshost** into the provided field, and then pressing Enter to run the service.

After this service is running, you can connect to the virtual base unit via any PC or server running Microsoft Response Point Administrator or Microsoft Response Point Assistant as if you were connecting to the hardware Base Unit device.

The benefit of this solution is for trainers like me who provide a lot of demos and do not want to carry all the required hardware for an actual on-site demonstration. The problem with this solution is that you are not able to leverage some of the firmware capabilities that the OEM manufacturers provide, such as Quanta/Syspine's built-in ATA adapters for analog phone support, the USB ports to run utilities such as the Password Reset, Erase Data, or System Info applications. But for me, that's not a problem because everything I want to use in Response Point does not require firmware. The Microsoft Response Point team has already confirmed that they will release a Softphone application for the Response Point system. At this point, I really do not see a future need for the physical hardware for me, personally, but I understand and heavily recommend OEM hardware for installations in small business or Small office/Home office (SoHo) environments where an IT administrator is not available to perform backup and restoration, or solve problems with the system as well as leverage the analog/PSTN gateway and physical phone devices in these on-premise locations.

But, just think how cool it is to know that you can fit the power of a IP-PBX that provides voice services for up to 50 people in an office in the size of something that fits in your palm! And it literally does! The CF Flash card like the one shown in Figure 10.4 is what Response Point's power VoIP features are running on.

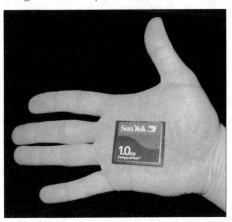

**FIGURE 10.4** The power of voice in the palm of your hand (Response Point Software)

Now, call me crazy, but that's innovation!

Response Point truly adds value long-term by providing a completely virtualized environment by enabling a virtual PBX and Softphone application for client use, completely wiping out the competition in the market as it exists today.

## The End of Telephony-Based Hardware

In November of 2008, I assisted Nortel with a case study integration research project that focused on Microsoft's Open Interoperatability Program. This program was created by Microsoft to create direct communication between Microsoft's Office Communication Server and widely used PBX systems from manufacturers including Nortel, Cisco, Avaya, Mitel, Siemens, and others. Nortel's Communication Server 1000 (CS1000) PBX was the first system on the list due to the heavy investment made by Microsoft into Nortel in 2005 with the Microsoft | Nortel Innovative Communications Alliance (ICA). The project was sponsored by Nortel as a reaction to Cisco's entry to this list—their newly announced upgrade of their Cisco Unified Communications Manager (CUCM) 7.0 release. Based on Cisco's marketing, CUCM 7.0 would provide direct communication to the Microsoft Office Communications Server in the same way that Nortel and Mitel provide it, without the need for a media gateway in between this connection. The tasks of this project included installing both a Nortel CS1000 PBX and a Cisco CUCM 7.0 system within our Evangelyze Communications test datacenter in Houston, Texas. During this project, we were commissioned to document differences based on level of installation complexity, TCO, and to document our personal opinions, as third-party field experts, of the differences between both systems.

To be honest, all I could think about was the waste of human time and physical space that both these solutions required. In 2010, Microsoft will upgrade and release a full-feature software-powered PBX system running within the Microsoft Office Communications Server (unless they change the name again). I really wish it was here now and not then. This way we could kill the Microsoft "VoIP as You Are" marketing campaign, and simply trash these ridiculous hardware-based PBX systems. The amount of effort to rack, power, network, and configure these systems using archaic cabling and confusing 400-page diagrams is beyond me. I felt as if I was stepping back in time and trying to troubleshoot a telegraph.

Figures 10.5 through 10.8 depict the test Cisco and Nortel PBX environment in our Evangelyze Communications datacenter in Houston, Texas.

**FIGURE 10.5** Nortel CS1000 (two Nortel MG1000 racks)

**FIGURE 10.6** Nortel CS1000 Blade inside one of the MG1000 racks

**FIGURE 10.7** Remaining Nortel CS1000 Configuration (Media Card and Signaling Server Blades)

**FIGURE 10.8** Dell PowerEdge Servers running Cisco CUCM environment

The definite con from a Nortel perspective was the annoying amount of hardware and the 350-page manual that came with the system. The nice thing was that after the configuration was completed, we only gained the ability to dual-fork incoming calls to enable the Microsoft Office Communicator simultaneous ring feature as mentioned in Chapter 4, "Enterprise Voice with Microsoft Unified Communications." As a team, we liked the fact that we could install the Cisco CUCM environment within our existing server environment. However, the Cisco software is only approved to run on IBM and HP hardware; after finding our Dell server MAC addresses, we were forced to run the software in a Virtual Machine software environment. The problem was that we were not running Windows at this point; we were running virtual Linux-based installations, which caused additional unnecessary software integration steps to make the configuration work. However, the Cisco environment only took us 3 hours to complete. Another example of the power of software! At this point, there is not enough approved documentation to show you how the software-powered PBX will make such a huge difference. But hopefully my experience and the photos will help you start to understand why software-powered voice services are so important.

## The Partner Opportunity for Voice Software Services

From a Microsoft partner perspective, voice services is the main area where money and time need to be invested now, because providing software-powered voice services will be the focal point in the Unified Communications industry within the next 5 years. My vision is that within the 2015 timeframe, smart organizations will begin to host voice services for their customers and provide linkage to voice services in the cloud through ITSP providers, bypassing FCC and other government regulatory requirements. Within this partner model, these organizations will be able to not only host outsourced voice solutions for their customers, but also extend vertical industry-focused voice applications to these customers as well. What this means is that a hosting provider such as Dell or HP could run Microsoft's Unified Communications platform to host the PBX and other calling features, as well as Microsoft Office SharePoint Portal Server, Live Meeting, and Exchange Server. This would provide the customer with all their hosted communication needs from a datacenter running only Microsoft Windows Server Hyper-V terminals. They could overlay these voice and collaboration services with applications that integrate into their customer's specific business processes whether they are in healthcare, legal, government, energy, financial, or other business verticals.

This transparency allows these hosting providers to also connect their customers with their business partners as well as other entities in a more seamless way than ever before, almost or hopefully eliminating the need for phone numbers. They could reach individuals based on name or expertise across all their communication devices. This means no more server hardware needed on-premise or onsite at the customer's location except for whatever communication devices they desire.

Figure 10.9 provides an example of how existing PBX manufacturers and Telco providers can start incorporating software and services and, thus, increase their market share in data services while depleting their existing hardware-based telephony devices which will be outdated by the year 2015.

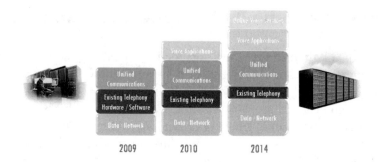

2009        2010        2014

**FIGURE 10.9** Joe Schurman's Unified Communications 5-Year Partner Model

By focusing on this transition, these organizations can create new services and software business that capitalizes on their telephony experience and existing customer base. Bottom-line cost issues that plague organizations, including power consumption, hardware costs, and consulting expertise and administration, could be solved to keep these existing hardware-based telephony solutions running. What I am spending time on now more than ever is trying to relay this vision to these existing Telco providers so that they can leverage their existing customer base and extend their business revenue to focus on software-powered voice, hosting voice services, and developing and integrating innovative business-process, communications, and collaboration-enabled applications.

Figure 10.10 depicts this new architecture of software-powered voice services and applications.

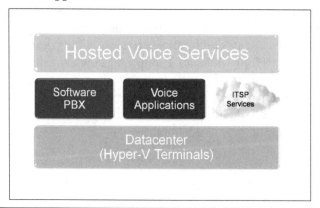

**FIGURE 10.10** Voice Software + Services architecture

For those who listen, they could triple their business revenue stream, drive innovation, and further continue what Gurdeep Singh Pall calls the "Communications Renaissance" to the future of Microsoft's vision of Software + Services!

## Virtual Resources

In addition to making Microsoft Virtual PC and Microsoft Hyper-V free to customers, Microsoft has compiled and published a lot of documentation and has also provided many sample Hyper-V and Virtual PC images for download. For more information on Windows Server 2008 Hyper-V, visit http://www.microsoft.com/hyperv. For more information on Microsoft Virtual PC, visit http://www.microsoft.com/virtualpc.

# CLOSING COMMENTS AND RESOURCES

First, I would like to thank you for taking the time to read some or all of this book. I have waited a long time to publish something like this, and I hope that you benefit from the understanding of what is written in this text. I have been lucky to work with Microsoft side by side since the beginning of the Real Time Collaboration and now Unified Communications Group. I also have been privileged and honored to work with Microsoft Research over the past couple of years launching Microsoft Response Point.

This is an exciting time for Microsoft Voice and Unified Communications products and services, and I am happy to have been there since the start of it all. It's interesting to stop for a second and look over at some of the people I have worked with at some of our industry events each year and see, just in a look and expression on their face, the feeling of accomplishment and awe of what has become of such an initially small community of resources and people.

It is my hope that in reading this book, you will understand why Microsoft is such an important player within the communications industry and how software-powered voice solutions will transform the way we communicate forever. You are only seeing the extreme early stages of this innovation by removing hardware-based telecommunications dependencies. Over the next 10 years, you will see a much more rapid launch of new communication devices, but more importantly, the ability to influence and enable business processes and line of business applications with voice and collaboration functionality, really transforming industries altogether. This is the Communications Renaissance Gurdeep spoke of in his foreword for this book. It is my vision that software and services will revolutionize the communications industry, and it is my hope that key Telco providers in these industries listen wisely or they will be replaced and forgotten in a very short period of time!

I am excited about the future of Microsoft's Voice and Unified Communications products and hope to continue to be a key influencer of this technology moving forward and hope to continue speaking at events to give customers, partners, and Microsoft representatives around the world the readiness information they need to understand and sell, the future of Microsoft Voice! I invite you to keep an eye out for upcoming Microsoft launch events and take part in as many as possible. The Microsoft marketing and business group is actually doing an unbelievable job in showcasing these new technologies and this vision of software plus services in the communications industry. Don't miss out, and take care.

Sincerely,
Joe Schurman,
Founder and CEO of Evangelyze Communications,
Microsoft MVP (Unified Communications Research)

# Resources

A lot of the content referenced in this book links to online resources available via the Web. To aid in the consolidation of some of these resources, we have created a Web site dedicated to this book via http://www.whatdouc.com to help you easily view and download content referenced in the book as well as other useful material to help you in your journey in working with Microsoft Voice and Unified Communications technologies.

In addition to the resource Web site, please use the Facebook global group called "Microsoft Voice and Unified Communications" at www.facebook.com to connect with others, view upcoming events, videos, and pictures, and to participate in the discussion board.

# INDEX

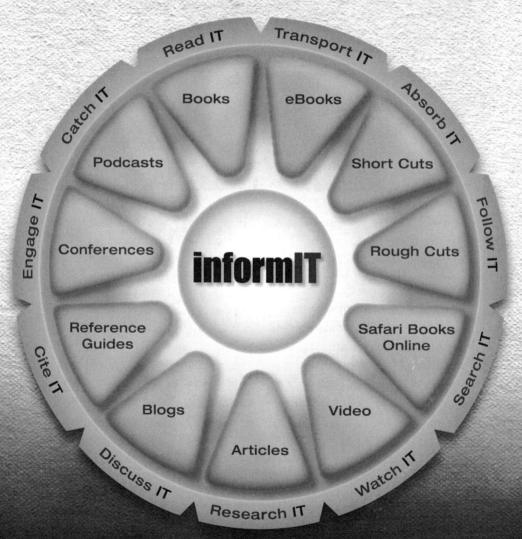

# Go Beyond the Book

Read IT

Transport IT

Catch IT

Absorb IT

Books

eBooks

Engage IT

Podcasts

Short Cuts

Follow IT

Conferences

**informIT**

Rough Cuts

Reference
Guides

Safari Books
Online

Search IT

Cite IT

Blogs

Video

Discuss IT

Articles

Watch IT

Research IT

**11 WAYS TO LEARN IT** at **www.informIT.com/learn**

The online portal of the information technology
publishing imprints of Pearson Education

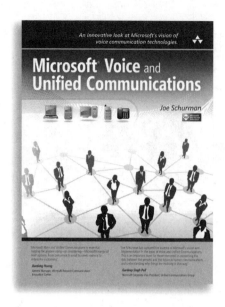

# FREE Online Edition

Your purchase of **Microsoft® Voice and Unified Communications** includes access to a free online edition for 120 days through the Safari Books Online subscription service. Nearly every Addison-Wesley Professional book is available online through Safari Books Online, along with more than 5,000 other technical books and videos from publishers such as Cisco Press, Exam Cram, IBM Press, O'Reilly, Prentice Hall, Que, and Sams.

**SAFARI BOOKS ONLINE** allows you to search for a specific answer, cut and paste code, download chapters, and stay current with emerging technologies.

## Activate your FREE Online Edition at www.informit.com/safarifree

> **STEP 1:** Enter the coupon code: EXCGKEH.

> **STEP 2:** New Safari users, complete the brief registration form.
> Safari subscribers, just log in.

If you have difficulty registering on Safari or accessing the online edition, please e-mail customer-service@safaribooksonline.com